W9-ADJ-597

L.W. Nixon Library
Butler Community College
901 South Haverhill Road
El Dorado, Kansas 67042-3280

At Issue

Are Adoption Policies Fair?

Other Books in the At Issue Series:

At Issue

Are Adoption Policies Fair?

Christine Watkins, Book Editor

GREENHAVEN PRESS
A part of Gale, Cengage Learning

Detroit • New York • San Francisco • New Haven, Conn • Waterville, Maine • London

Elizabeth Des Chenes, *Director, Publishing Solutions*

© 2012 Greenhaven Press, a part of Gale, Cengage Learning.

Gale and Greenhaven Press are registered trademarks used herein under license.

For more information, contact:
Greenhaven Press
27500 Drake Rd.
Farmington Hills, MI 48331-3535
Or you can visit our Internet site at gale.cengage.com

ALL RIGHTS RESERVED.
No part of this work covered by the copyright herein may be reproduced, transmitted, stored, or used in any form or by any means graphic, electronic, or mechanical, including but not limited to photocopying, recording, scanning, digitizing, taping, Web distribution, information networks, or information storage and retrieval systems, except as permitted under Section 107 or 108 of the 1976 United States Copyright Act, without the prior written permission of the publisher.

For product information and technology assistance, contact us at

Gale Customer Support, 1-800-877-4253
For permission to use material from this text or product, submit all requests online at www.cengage.com/permissions.

Further permissions questions can be e-mailed to permissionrequest@cengage.com.

Articles in Greenhaven Press anthologies are often edited for length to meet page requirements. In addition, original titles of these works are changed to clearly present the main thesis and to explicitly indicate the author's opinion. Every effort is made to ensure that Greenhaven Press accurately reflects the original intent of the authors. Every effort has been made to trace the owners of copyrighted material.

Cover image © Images.com/Corbis.

LIBRARY OF CONGRESS CATALOGING-IN-PUBLICATION DATA

Are adoption policies fair? / Christine Watkins, book editor.
    p. cm. -- (At issue)
Includes bibliographical references and index.
ISBN 978-0-7377-6147-4 (hbk.) -- ISBN 978-0-7377-6148-1 (pbk.)
1. Adoption--United States--Juvenile literature. 2. Adoption--Government policy--United States--Juvenile literature. 3. Adopted children--United States--Juvenile literature. 4. Adoption agencies--United States--Juvenile literature. I. Watkins, Christine, 1951-
    HV875.55.A742 2012
    362.7340973--dc23
                                                                          2012008666

Printed in the United States of America
1 2 3 4 5 6 7 16 15 14 13 12

Contents

Introduction

According to the US Children's Bureau report "Trends in Foster Care and Adoption—FY2002–FY2010," America has approximately 662,000 children in foster care, many of whom end up in the system as a result of abuse or neglect by their parents. For example, in October 2011 five children were placed in foster care after their parents, Anthony and Tammy Irvin, were arrested and accused of beating the children with electrical cords, locking them in a closet and the garage, and depriving them of food and water for days at a time. In other situations, children are removed from their homes because their parents have substance abuse problems, or because they lack the necessary resources or abilities to nurture and care for their children. Oftentimes poverty is the catalyst. In most cases when children are taken by a county's Social Services Department, the intent is to reunify them with their biological parents or families once the abusive or neglectful behavior has been corrected. And therein lies a dilemma. Before a foster child can be adopted into a permanent home, the rights of the biological parents must be legally terminated. The question becomes: How much time should parents be given for rehabilitation before their children can become eligible for adoption? Is one year too soon? Is five years too long? Most people agree it is only right that biological parents be given the opportunity to reform or recover and redeem their parental rights. But for many children languishing in the foster care system, and for hopeful potential adoptive parents, the length of time involved in the process can seem overly long.

The majority of experts and child advocates believe it is in children's best interests to be restored to their biological families. In fact, slightly more than half of all children who enter foster care do return to their birth families. Additionally, many child-placement professionals believe that more resources and support services—such as parenting classes— should be made available to struggling and vulnerable families to prevent children from entering the foster care system in the first place. As Judith Sandalow, executive director of the Children's Law Center in Washington, DC, told the US Senate in March, 2010, "Removing children from their homes—even abusive or neglectful homes—is an inherently traumatizing action ... These traumatic removals should only occur as a last resort, when prevention and support services are unable to prevent children from being harmed in their homes." And statistics have shown that after foster children reach the age of eighteen, many search out their biological parents, relatives, or siblings in hopes of reuniting, offering further evidence of the innate longing for family connection.

Yet despite the goal of family reunification, state agencies and advocacy groups have come to recognize the damage done to children who spend much of their childhood moving from one temporary setting to another while waiting for their parents to progress through necessary requirements in order to regain custody of their children. In the meantime, "with multiple placements and growing older, these children ultimately become increasingly 'unadoptable' or difficult to adopt through no fault of their own," writes Mario Salazar in the September 16, 2011, *Washington Times* article "Foster Children Need Loving Homes." And all too often during the drawn-out process, the children "age out," which means they become ineligible to remain in foster care because of their age (eighteen in most states), and are left to live on their own. In their September 2008 Policy Brief for the Evan B. Donaldson Adoption Institute "Expanding Resources for Waiting Children II," Jeanne Howard and Madelyn Freundlich explained the consequences of aging out. "While youths in the general population continue to rely on family long after they reach 18 ... those who have spent years in foster care because they experienced abuse and neglect are expected to become independent and self-sufficient in late adolescence. These youths, lacking permanent families to help them transition into adulthood, are at heightened risk of negative outcomes: emotional adjustment problems, poor educational results and employment prospects, and inadequate housing and homelessness; furthermore, they are more likely to become involved with the criminal justice system." Thus, for children in foster care, delays can be disastrous.

Returning to the original question, how much time should biological parents be given before their parental rights are terminated? No definitive answer has been reached among experts, and the passionate debate continues. There seems to be a general consensus, however, that the permanency and stability needs of a child should be considered paramount. As Adam Pertman wrote in his book *Adoption Nation: How the Adoption Revolution Is Transforming Our Families—and America,* federal and state governments are "revising the nation's social-work and judicial objective from single-minded 'family preservation' to 'timely permanence.'" Also, to minimize the emotional stress from disrupting a child's life, social workers, child professionals, and family court judges are offering compromises, such as encouraging family visitation or the use of open adoptions, in which adopted children can maintain contact with their birth families.

The authors in *At Issue: Are Adoption Policies Fair?* discuss foster children, open adoption, and many other issues concerning the legal, moral, and practical aspects of adoption policies.

1

Open Adoptions Benefit Society

Adam Pertman

Adam Pertman is the executive director of the Evan B. Donaldson Adoption Institute and the associate editor of Adoption Quarterly, *an international journal that examines adoption issues.*

In the past, adoptions were typically kept secret, often leaving those involved—adoptees, adoptive parents, and birth parents (the triad)—with lifelong feelings of shame and guilt. Increasingly, however, adoptions have become more open, making it easier to reunite adoptees with birth parents, give adoptees vital medical and historical information, and rewrite laws so that single people, middle-aged couples, and gay men and lesbians can become parents and provide loving homes for children. Although this "adoption revolution" is still evolving and certain issues need to be resolved, the growing awareness and acceptance of adoption undeniably benefits those specifically involved and society as a whole.

After a long period of warning tremors, adoption is "changing" like a simmering volcano changes when it can no longer contain its explosive energy: It erupts. The hot lava flows from its core, permanently reshaping not only the mountain itself but also every inch of landscape it touches. The new

Adam Pertman, *Adoption Nation: How the Adoption Revolution Is Transforming Our Families—and America*, 2nd Edition. Boston, MA: Harvard Common Press, 2011, pp. 5–8, 14–17. Copyright © 2011 by Harvard Common Press. All rights reserved. Reproduced by permission.

earth becomes more fertile, richer in color. The sensation of watching the transformation, of being a part of it, is an awesome amalgam of anxiety and exhilaration. The metamorphosis itself is breathtaking. Before our eyes, in our homes and schools and media and workplaces, America is forever changing adoption even as adoption is forever changing America.

A Revolution of Openness and Acceptance

This is nothing less than a revolution. After decades of incremental improvements and tinkering at the margins, adoption is reshaping itself to the core. It is shedding its corrosive stigmas and rejecting its secretive past; states are revising their laws and agencies are rewriting their rules even as the Internet is rendering them obsolete, especially by making it simpler for adoptees and birth parents to find each other; single women, multiracial families, and gay men and lesbians are flowing into the parenting mainstream; middle-aged couples are bringing a rainbow of children from abroad into their predominantly white communities; and social-service agencies are making it far easier to find homes for hundreds of thousands of children whose short lives have been squandered in the foster-care system.

It's not just that adoption suddenly seems to be appearing everywhere at once, as if revealed by a cosmic sleight of hand. Society's acceptance—and even embrace—of it is also growing. The new climate allows birth parents like the actresses Mercedes Ruehl, Roseanne Barr, and Kate Mulgrew, the singers Joni Mitchell and David Crosby, along with thousands of men and women unprotected by famous names, to finally ease their torment by disclosing their secrets and meeting their children. It leads celebrities like Hugh Jackman, Angelina Jolie, Steven Spielberg, Tom Cruise, and Rosie O'Donnell to proudly announce the arrival of their adopted children, further raising the profile of the process and accelerating public understanding that it's another normal way of forming a family. And it allows adoptees to learn that they aren't "different" in any negative sense, though they've been treated that way in the past; rather, they're part of a big, successful community whose members range from baseball legend Jim Palmer to former President Gerald Ford to Apple Computer founder Steve Jobs to rap music pioneer Darryl (DMC) McDaniels.

Stunningly, marvelously, for the first time in its history, adoption has come into vogue. At a dinner party with a half-dozen friends, I once offhandedly cited a well-known statistic among researchers—that only about 1 percent of American women relinquish their babies for adoption today, a precipitous drop from a few decades ago—to which one woman at the table responded: "Are you sure it isn't much higher? Just about everyone I know with children adopted them." A few weeks later, an acquaintance told me that a classmate of her nine-year-old son, upon learning that he was adopted, sounded downright envious. "That's so cool," the boy said, and none of the other kids huddled around them offered a hint of dissent.

Every historic phenomenon begins with a specific group and then sweeps through the entire population. That's what is happening in America today, complete with the trepidation and triumph that accompany all cultural upheavals. The emerging new realities undeniably are replete with problems and paradoxes. They are raising new issues for families and creating new dilemmas for the country. But they also are more sensible, more humane, and more focused on children's well-being than the realities being left behind.

Adoption is at once a marvel of humanity and a social safety valve. It permits the infertile among us to share the deeply fulfilling, profoundly joyful experience of raising children. It offers a positive option for people who, for moral or economic or personal reasons, believe they can neither undergo an abortion nor parent a child. Most important, whatever it might accomplish for the adults in the picture, it provides a systematic opportunity for children to grow up in stable homes with loving parents.

The revolution was long overdue, and it already is having a penetrating impact. It is advancing the ethnic, racial, and cultural diversity that is a hallmark of twenty-first-century America, and it is contributing to a permanent realignment in the way we think of family structure. It is a revolution reflected in our national and state politics, in our newspapers and on the World Wide Web, even in the ads we watch on television. And it promises to help heal one of our most virulent national diseases: the withering away of children in foster care.

Americans can feel something happening around them, and even *to* them, but most haven't identified the revolution for what it is. They assume, as we all mistakenly do about so many aspects of life, that only the people directly involved in adoption are affected by it. Americans are too busy or distracted to consider why they haven't been aware of the adoptees, adoptive parents, and birth parents in their midst (and they certainly wouldn't talk about it if they were), yet suddenly they see us everywhere they turn

A History of Secrecy

Of course, we were always there. But our existence was carefully cloaked, just as the history of adoption itself has been written, and hidden, in the shadows. Sadly, for too many generations, this wonderful and vexing process diminished nearly everyone in its embrace, even as it served their needs or transformed their lives.

Too many of adoption's ostensible beneficiaries, adoptive parents, spent decades deceiving those they cherished most; they often didn't reveal their children's origins at all or insisted they share the truth with no one. Adoption's most essential participants, birth parents, were dehumanized; they were forced to bury their grief and humiliation within themselves, unable to share their burden with even their closest confidants. And this domestic drama's most vulnerable-players, adoptees, the only ones with no say in the decision that defined their existence, were relegated to second-class social and legal status; in perhaps the most insidiously demeaning act of all, even very young adoptees were made to understand that exploring this fundamental aspect of their beings was taboo.

[T]here are at least 7 million adopted children and adults in the United States today . . .

Not a very healthy state of affairs for an institution that was supposed to help people, which adoption most often has done despite its flaws. But now the revolution is upon us. Adoption is emerging into the warm, if sometimes harsh, light of day. It is changing rapidly, radically, and for the better. It's not quite a caterpillar shedding its cocoon, emerging as a flawless, beautiful butterfly. Light reveals imperfections, after all, and sometimes it even causes them. Still, the darkness was a far gloomier place to be, and problems that we see are easier to deal with and resolve than those that remain hidden.

Ironically, one thing we are learning as we realize how widespread adoption has become is that generations of secrecy prevent us from knowing just how widespread it truly is. The subject has been considered off-limits for so long, both by individuals and by society as a whole, that until very recently studies have not been devised, census questions have not been asked, surveys have not been conducted. There is no national organization or branch of government that keeps track of adoptions, so determining how many "triad" [adoptees, adoptive parents, birth parents] members there are—or have been—would require sorting through the individual "finalization" records in every courthouse in every city and town in every state.

Extrapolating from U.S. Census data, we can guesstimate that there are at least 7 million adopted children and adults in the United States today, add in birth parents, adoptive parents, grandparents, siblings, uncles and aunts, and nephews and nieces, and the number of people directly connected to adoption soars into the tens of millions. And many experts believe the number is even larger, because an incalculable percentage of adoptees still don't know they were adopted, and many people in what I call the extended family of adoption—meaning adopted children and adults, birth and adoptive parents, siblings, and so on—continue to mislead anyone who asks, as well as themselves. . . .

The Many Benefits of Openness

First and foremost, social-work and mental-health experts have reached a consensus that greater openness offers an array of benefits for adoptees—from ongoing information about family medical issues to fulfillment of their innate desire to know about their genealogical histories—even if the expanded relationships prove difficult or complicated for some of the participants.

At the same time, adoption professionals are coming to terms with a stark truth about birth mothers, particularly those of past generations: The vast majority did not "forget and get on with their lives," as though they were machines built to incubate life and give it away. In fact, most of these women experienced some level of emotional and psychic injury, no matter how good they considered their reasons to be or how much denial they permitted themselves. Overwhelmingly, later in life if not right away, whether they say so out loud or only whisper the truth to themselves in the protective darkness of sleepless nights, most yearn for contact with or knowledge about their children.

Adoption is supposed to help people, not torment them. So, as the consequences of the old ways have become clear, adoption agencies and attorneys who arrange "closed" adoptions have become an endangered species. It's a remarkable reversal from the standard operating procedure of past decades, when all identifying data about birth and adoptive parents were guarded like nuclear secrets—and the very idea of a face-to-face meeting was considered perverse. "What's wrong with her? Why can't she just get on with her life?" social workers asked if a birth mother hinted she'd like to know how her baby was doing. Adoptees and adoptive parents were viewed as ungrateful, perhaps even unstable, if they sought information about the people who made their families possible.

Some birth parents still seek confidentiality, and a small percentage presumably always will, because of their personalities or personal circumstances. But as society and the adoption system permit them to feel less guilt and shame about their decisions, the ranks of the anonymous are dwindling. Most often now, it's the adoptive mothers and fathers who are apprehensive about openness—though, again, in smaller and smaller numbers.

[A]ll of the people involved become more secure when their relationships cease to be based on fear and fantasy.

Caution and protectiveness are understandable emotions for anyone with normal instincts and insecurities, but all the more so for most adoptive parents. Our sensitivities about raising a family usually have been heightened by fertility problems that have prevented us from producing biological children, and our self-confidence has been further shaken by the emotionally turbulent voyage that adoption too often entails. As hard as it may be to accept, however, the adoptive parents' gut-level concerns about the consequences of openness are typically exaggerated and usually unfounded.

Most reassuring is the fact that there's no clinical or practical evidence to indicate that adoptees or birth parents try to disrupt or interfere with adoptions that include sustained contact. To the contrary, many adoptive families grow stronger, and all of the people involved become more secure, when their relationships cease to be based on fear and fantasy.

Besides, in the vast majority of cases, the adoptive parents are the gatekeepers. They decide the extent and timing of any participation in open relationships, or even knowledge about birth relatives, by their children. While adoptees generally are curious, and ask more and more questions as they get older, they typically don't request detailed information or consider the possibility of in-person meetings (unless these have already occurred) until they are into their teens. And adoptees seldom seek out their biological parents before they are well into their twenties or thirties, when planning for their own futures often heightens their desire to know more about their pasts—though, with the advent of social media like Facebook, the number of younger searchers is rising.

An Evolving Process

That's the current, fading snapshot. But, like everything else about adoption, the new picture still hasn't come into focus. Every day, more and more adoptive mothers and fathers are making contact with birth parents while their children are still very small. Adoptees are exploring their roots at younger and younger ages, empowered in part by the extraordinary resources of the Internet, while birth mothers, fathers, siblings, and sometimes whole families are increasingly summoning the courage to search for and develop relationships with their biological sons, daughters, brothers, and sisters.

There undeniably are complexities and difficulties in "open adoption," an imprecise term applied to an array of arrangements in which birth parents stay involved after placing a child. Some problems derive from the specific personalities or situations of those involved, but many are characteristic of various phases of the relationship as everyone tries to deal with emotional uncertainty and, if direct contact is included, to determine their boundaries and sort out their evolving roles. In most cases the long-term gains are considerable nevertheless, and that's why expanding openness is the central characteristic of the adoption revolution. . . .

2

International Adoptions Need Stronger Regulations

E.J. Graff

E.J. Graff is an associate director and senior researcher at Brandeis University's Schuster Institute for Investigative Journalism.

Many Americans have the best intentions when adopting children from other countries, often believing they are rescuing orphans from adverse conditions. But there is a hidden side of international adoption that often includes fraud, corruption, or even kidnapping. Because the demand for babies has skyrocketed, Americans are willing to pay thousands of dollars in adoption fees in order to adopt a child from an underdeveloped country. Looking to make a fortune in the adoption market, unscrupulous brokers lie to or coerce families into giving up or selling their children; in some cases children are kidnapped to be sold to American parents. The Hague Convention is a good start at prohibiting child marketing, but more must be done to ensure the welfare and parental care of vulnerable children worldwide.

When Katie and Calvin Bradshaw adopted three young sisters from Ethiopia in 2006, they believed they were saving AIDS orphans from a life of poverty or near-certain prostitution. But after learning English, the girls told their new parents that they believed the adoption agency, Christian World Adoption, had paid their birthfather for them. The girls

E.J. Graff, "The Baby Business: U.S. Couples Adopting from Abroad Often Think They're Helping Vulnerable Children. The Reality Is More Complex—and Poorly Regulated," *Democracy: A Journal of Ideas*, Issue 17, Summer 2010. Copyright © 2010 by Democracy: A Journal of Ideas, Inc. All rights reserved. Reproduced by permission.

said they had expected to return to their extended Ethiopian family, who were middle-class by local standards, as both CBS News and Australia's ABC News reported. The Bradshaws were rightly horrified. (Today, the two younger girls are still with them, while the oldest daughter lives with Katie Bradshaw's mother; in a lengthy response to the CBS News report, Christian World Adoption said it had no contact with the girls' birth family).

Marketing Children

I've heard a string of similar tales from families in Italy, Canada, Austria, and other Western countries adopting from Ethiopia, the current hot adoption source. In the past five years, Ethiopia's adoptions to the United States alone have expanded exponentially: Americans adopted 442 Ethiopian children in 2005, and 2,277 in 2009, ranking Ethiopia right behind China as a source for our international adoptions. The combination of skyrocketing numbers and troubling stories suggests that Ethiopia has become the latest country beset by an all-too-common problem: a poor country in which unscrupulous middlemen are sometimes buying, defrauding, coercing, or even kidnapping children away from their families to be sold into international adoption.

[I]nternational adoption has been a Wild West, all but free of meaningful law, regulation, or oversight.

Most nations' adoption programs are relatively clean. But during some periods, in some countries—Cambodia between 1997 and 2002, for instance, or Vietnam between 2005 and 2009—evidence from government, newspaper, and NGO [nongovernmental organization] investigations strongly suggests that many international adoptions involved fraud. Serious problems have also been documented in such countries as Liberia, Nepal, the Marshall Islands, Peru, Samoa, and most notably, Guatemala, whose processes were so riddled with corruption that it was finally closed to adoption in 2009, after 10 years during which Americans adopted more than 30,000 of its children, in some years bringing home an astonishing one of every 100 babies born there.

Large-hearted Westerners—eager to fill out their families while helping a child in need—have adopted tens of thousands of children from these and other poor countries. Very few are aware of this heartbreaking underside of international adoption—and many have trouble believing it when they do hear such stories. But the fact is that for decades, international adoption has been a Wild West, all but free of meaningful law, regulation, or oversight. In the past ten years, upward of 20,000 Western families each year have adopted internationally. Tens of thousands more are on waiting lists for years. Western adoption agencies, seeking to satisfy demand, have poured millions of dollars of adoption fees into underdeveloped countries. Those dollars and Euros have, too often, induced the unscrupulous to take children away from families that loved and would have raised them to adulthood. Corruption skips from one unprepared country to another—until that country gets wise, changes its laws, and corrupt adoptions shift to the next unprepared nation.

Understanding the Real Problem

Such corruption can happen in part because American perception and policy about orphans have been distorted by a fundamental myth. Many people believe that millions of healthy babies need Western homes, lest they wither in institutions or die on the streets. This myth is perpetuated, to some extent, by UNICEF's [United Nations Children's Fund] misleading estimate that the world includes 163 million orphans. It's not so. Most of UNICEF's "orphans" are "single" orphans, having lost just one parent; others live with extended family. Most children in need of international adoption are older than five, sick, disabled, or otherwise traumatized. Many Westerners find it counterintuitive, even impossible, that the world isn't filled with healthy babies needing Western families. It's certainly true that millions of children are in desperate straits in benighted parts of the world: stacked up in brutal institutions in former Soviet bloc countries; roaming the streets in African cities; scavenging from Latin American trash heaps; enslaved in gravel pits in South Asia. Some of these children do need new homes abroad—because their families have failed, their health needs are extreme, their communities have cast them out, or because of unusual conditions like China's one-child policy or the Communist legacy of institutionalization (in which workers were encouraged to let their children be raised by the state, in what proved to be horrific institutions). Quite understandably, fewer Westerners are prepared to take in the older, ill, or more challenging children. And so they put their names down for the healthy babies they believe are available.

[S]ome entrepreneurial locals saw ways to make money from Westerners' good intentions.

Ending corruption in international adoption may seem like an obscure and narrow issue, but its implications reach throughout child welfare and development efforts worldwide. What's the right way to help children after the Haitian earthquake or the Liberian civil war? How can the United States help African AIDS orphans become productive citizens instead of pirates or insurgents? What is international adoption's correct role in child welfare? The answers are linked. What the United States needs now are improved policies, practices, and regulations that simultaneously help prevent the criminal underside of the adoption trade and support child welfare and protection systems, so that impoverished families and disrupted communities can keep most of their children home.

Already in place are a treaty, a law, sets of regulations, and a host of aid efforts on behalf of children. But significant gaps remain. Plugging some important holes—and heightening our investments in, and coordination of, services that help children stay with their families—would go a long way toward saving children from being wrongfully taken from their birth families, and Americans from later discovering that they unwittingly paid someone to buy them a child.

The Hague Convention on Intercountry Adoption

The international community woke up to unethical adoptions in the late 1980s and early 1990s. In 1989, the United Nations enacted the Convention on the Rights of the Child (CRC), which included principles about preventing wrongful international adoptions. But the need for still more protections became clear after Nicolae Ceausescu fell in 1989, exposing Romania's brutal warehouses of orphaned or abandoned children. Thousands of well-meaning Westerners flocked to Romania to bring home orphans. Predictably, some entrepreneurial locals saw ways to make money from Westerners' good intentions. By 1991, most American adoptions from Romania were coming not from institutions but from "facilitators" who solicited children directly from birth families in hospitals, on the streets, even in individual homes, in some cases while dumbstruck Westerners stood by.

In 1993, 66 countries, including the United States, gathered at the Hague Conference on Private International Law to create the Convention on Protection of Children and Co-Operation In Respect of Intercountry Adoption. To join the Hague Convention on Intercountry Adoption, as it is known, a nation must commit itself to cooperate "to prevent the abduction, the sale of, or traffic in children" for international adoption. The United States signed the treaty in 1994, ratified it in 2000, and implemented its requirements on April 1, 2008.

The 1993 Hague Convention's biggest gap is easy to identify: it allows signatories to continue adoptions outside the Hague system. Western signatories (including the United States, Italy, France, and Spain) can, and do, still permit adoption from the "non-Hague" countries that lack the treaty's protective systems. Of the world's 195 or so countries, only 81 have entered the Hague Convention. More than two-thirds of U.S. citizens' international adoptions come from "non-Hague" countries, including Russia, Korea, Kazakhstan, and Ethiopia. A number of countries outside the system have experienced significant adoption scandals. But according to Susan Soon-Keum Cox of Holt International Children's Services, a highly respected Oregon-based international adoption and child welfare group, who attended the conference that crafted it, the convention's "minimal standards" were as far as participants would go; pushing for more restrictions would have scuttled the treaty entirely.

The Hague Convention's overarching instruction commands signatories to take "all appropriate measures to prevent improper financial or other gain . . . and to deter all practices contrary" to the goal of ending trafficking for adoption. Toward that end, each Hague Convention country must have a "central authority"—a government body—that oversees international adoptions. The central authority's tasks differ, depending on whether that country is on the supply or demand side (let's oversimplify and call them "poor" or "wealthy" countries) of international adoption.

The convention's "subsidiarity" principle declares that keeping children with their original families should be the top child-welfare priority. This implies that each nation should have child-welfare and protection systems, social services, and other supports to help families stay together despite financial, medical, or other kinds of distress. That's a big investment for poor countries, and it holds some back from joining the treaty. Other nations remain outside Hague because of national political concerns about sovereignty; still others, such as Nepal, are not committed to ending corruption, according to a report from the Hague Permanent Bureau. When original families are unfit, the convention urges nations to try to place the child with kin, neighbors, or others within the country, saving the child from the trauma of total relocation. Only as a last resort—to keep a child out of institutions, for instances—should the nation refer a child for international adoption, and then only to foreign adoption agencies that it has screened and licensed.

The adopting countries are also charged with creating "central authorities," whose tasks involve certifying that the prospective adopting families are prepared to be good parents, and assessing that whoever will be working on adoption is ethical, competently trained, has nonprofit goals, and maintains sound business practices. Central authorities on both sides are supposed to communicate directly, in part to keep Western adoption agencies from contracting directly with poor nations' orphanages or "facilitators."

International adoption shouldn't be a way of finding children for families; it should be a way of finding families for children.

Some countries reputed to have the best "Hague systems" excelled before signing, or without formally entering, the Hague adoption convention. Before signing the convention, for instance, Thailand and Colombia had centralized oversight of child-welfare programs, trained social workers, begun aiding families in distress, and installed oversight so that only children who have no other good options are offered to foreign families. And in other countries that have signed—India is the prime example—ongoing scandals suggest that the central authority may be either inept at screening out bad actors or perhaps corrupt. . . .

The biggest problem with the U.S. Hague implementation efforts is similar to the one that exists in the convention at large: the United States officially applies its "Hague" rules only to adoptions from other Hague nations. Which means that, for most American families seeking to adopt, full Hague safeguards do not apply. In fiscal year 2009, Americans adopted 12,753 children from other countries. Fewer than 4,000 of those came from countries that have entered the Hague Convention. Those numbers aren't as dire as they seem. Most non-Hague adoptions come either from "semi-Hague" countries—for instance, Russia won't license U.S. agencies unless they are Hague-accredited—or are arranged by Hague-accredited agencies. But U.S. agencies without Hague accreditation may nevertheless arrange adoptions from countries outside the Hague Convention—and can be found working in problem countries like Nepal and Ethiopia. . . .

Focusing on Child Welfare Worldwide

Preventing corrupt international adoptions won't happen simply through statutes, rules, and regulations. Children can be bought or stolen for adoption for the same reasons they're vulnerable to other horrors: dire poverty, ill health, plague, disaster, civil war, weak legal systems, and nonexistent social infrastructures. That's also why they can be bought or stolen for sex and labor; why they end up on the streets instead of in schools; why they are vulnerable to starvation, rape, HIV, homelessness, and other preventable diseases. International adoption shouldn't be a way of finding children for families; it should be a way of finding families for children. The Hague Convention offers tools to prevent, police, and prosecute crime and corruption related to international adoption. But children and their families need more than police and prosecutors; they need the teachers, nurses, and social workers who help prevent them from falling into danger in the first place. How should the United States help provide that affirmative aid?

A few years ago [2005], realizing that no one in Washington was tracking what the federal government spent to help children worldwide, Representative Barbara Lee, Democrat from California, sponsored a statute to track, add up, and coordinate all those different child-related aid efforts out of the government's octopal arms. The resulting Special Advisor on Orphans and Vulnerable Children (OVC) sits in USAID [United States Agency for International Development], and holds regular coordinating meetings with the federal staff and agencies that have invested in children's well-being in a myriad of ways. It includes the State Department's OCI [Office of Children's Issues] office, which handles Hague enforcement efforts, as well as the various offices that administer, say, micropayments for seeds and school uniforms, so that African grandmothers can feed and educate AIDS orphans instead of sending them to orphanages. It includes the USAID officers who worked with the Romanian government for more than 10 years to develop a workable child welfare system and culture in that country. Many international child welfare groups back this office's approach, and want to see it more fully funded.

Another Washington faction has also proposed a new diplomatic-level office at the State Department, akin to the Office to Monitor and Combat Trafficking in Persons, that would promote efforts to strengthen families worldwide: funding a census of orphans, assessing "best practices" in helping fragile and vulnerable families, and offering poor countries assistance in building the kind of social welfare infrastructures that would ease entry into the Hague Convention, in order to help ensure that every child in the world was being raised "in parental care." [Louisiana Democratic Senator Mary] Landrieu is sponsoring this bill. . . .

Given Secretary Hillary Clinton's dedication to the welfare of children, women, and families worldwide, her State Department should examine existing systems against these new proposals, including those in this article, to ensure that everything necessary is being done to keep families together during poverty, turmoil, and crisis. The Hague Convention on Intercountry Adoption is merely a legal regime to enable countries to transfer the relatively small percentage of children who need international homes. International adoption will never be the solution for all, or even most, of the world's vulnerable children. Tens of millions of children and their families, in desperate straits in their home countries, need and deserve assistance so that they can thrive in place. Defrauded birth families from Nepal, Vietnam, Cambodia, Guatemala, and Ethiopia may never see their children again. But surely the United States can work harder to see that such losses don't strike other families. When done right, international adoption is a last-ditch effort—not induced at the intersection of hope, greed, and poverty, but undertaken in the best interests of children.

3

Religious Groups Want to Increase International Adoptions

Kathryn Joyce

Kathryn Joyce is the author of Quiverfull: Inside the Christian Patriarchy Movement *and is presently working on a book about ethics and religion.*

With the goal of rescuing an imagined 145 million children worldwide as well as spreading the Christian gospel, religious leaders across America are promoting a "crusade to create a culture of adoption." The crusade, however, comes at a time when ethical scandals and accusations of child trafficking have led to tightened regulations for international adoptions. Undeterred, many evangelical adoption agencies defy these regulations by falsifying visas or committing other serious violations; they believe their adoption movement will transform the system and that expanding international adoptions is God's will.

In late March [2011] Craig Juntunen told a group of Christian adoption advocates assembled at a Chandler, Arizona, home about his plans to increase international adoptions fivefold. Just over a year before [2010], the world had been riveted by the saga of Laura Silsby, the American missionary arrested while trying to transport Haitian children across the Dominican border. But the lessons of that scandal seemed far from Juntunen's mind as he described his "crusade to create a

Kathryn Joyce, "The Evangelical Adoption Crusade," *The Nation*, May 9, 2011. Copyright © 2011 by The Nation. All rights reserved. Reproduced by permission.

culture of adoption" by simplifying adoption's labyrinthine ethical complexities to their emotional core. Juntunen, a former pro football quarterback and the adoptive father of three Haitian children, has emerged as a somewhat rogue figure in the adoption world since he recently founded an unorthodox nonprofit, Both Ends Burning. He has commissioned a documentary about desperate orphans in teeming institutions, *Wrongfully Detained,* and proposed a "clearinghouse model" that will raise the number of children adopted into US families to more than 50,000 per year.

A Crusade to Spread the Christian Gospel

Juntunen acknowledges that many adoption experts find his proposals naïve, particularly in a year that witnessed scandals in Haiti, Nepal and most recently Ethiopia, where widespread irregularities and trafficking allegations may slow the once-booming program to a crawl. He met a chilly reception recently at the Adoption Policy Conference at New York Law School when he spoke alongside State Department officials. But Juntunen insists that his ideas for increasing adoption constitute a social movement, akin to the civil rights movement, and that the force of a growing "adoption culture" will help them prevail.

In this expectation, he may be right. In Arizona, Juntunen was speaking with Dan Cruver, head of Together for Adoption, a key coalition in a growing evangelical adoption movement. The event was the first of the organization's new "house conferences": small-scale meet-ups bolstering an active national movement that promotes Christians' adopting as a way to address a worldwide "orphan crisis" they say encompasses hundreds of millions of children. It's a message Cruver also emphasizes in his book *Reclaiming Adoption*—one in a growing list of titles about "orphan theology," which teaches that adoption mirrors Christian salvation, plays an essential role in antiabortion politics and is a means of fulfilling the Great Commission, the biblical mandate that Christians spread the gospel.

Yet while Cruver and his colleagues have inspired thousands of Christians to enter the arduous and expensive process of international adoption, the adoption industry is on a steep decline after years of ethical problems and tightening regulations around the world. Since the mid-'90s, eighty-three countries have ratified the Hague convention regulating international adoption. By 2010 there were 12,000 such adoptions in the United States (including 1,100 exceptional "humanitarian parole" cases from post-earthquake Haiti)—almost half those at the peak in 2004. If evangelicals heed Culver's call en masse, it could mean not just a radical change in who raises the world's children but a powerful clash between rapidly falling supply and sharply inflating demand. . . .

After the Haiti earthquake, the evangelical adoption movement sprang into action. Next to longstanding religious relief orphanages, upstart evangelical missions appeared. Some flung themselves into adversarial activism, decrying international aid organizations like UNICEF [United Nations Children's Fund] for obstructing the speedy adoption of Haitian children.

Creating an "Adoption Culture"

In the United States, evangelicals and sympathetic politicians led the charge for expanded, expedited international adoption for what they had claimed before the earthquake was the country's 400,000 or more orphans—a figure repeated widely, despite a UNICEF clarification that likely only 50,000 children had lost both parents. (Identifying which children fit this description is a matter of painstaking investigation.)

Senator Mary Landrieu, a Louisiana Democrat and staunch adoption advocate, argued ferociously to expand a "humanitarian parole" program that expedites adoptions in progress:

"Either UNICEF is going to change or have a very difficult time getting support from the US Congress," she told the Associated Press.

Others used the emotional language of rescue; a Mormon mission president said he had "negotiated the release" of sixty-six children bound for Salt Lake City homes.

But what most people will remember about adoption in Haiti is the saga of Laura Silsby and nine other Southern Baptists who were jailed after trying to transport thirty-three "orphans"—most solicited from living families—to an unbuilt orphanage in the Dominican Republic, to await prospective evangelical adopters. Throughout the scandal the group members maintained they were simply "ten Christians who obeyed God's calling."

Churches report a "contagious" "adoption culture" in which even small congregations have adopted dozens of children in just a few years.

Silsby's claims to divine guidance attracted scorn from the media—one outlet accused her of "baby-snatching for Jesus"—but her language resonates with now-commonplace Christian adoption rhetoric.

The movement cuts across evangelical distinctions, with the Southern Baptists taking a doctrinal lead; charismatic prayer warrior Lou Engle, co-founder of TheCall, praying for "the most outrageous adoption movement to be released through the church"; and Rick Warren declaring that members of his Saddleback Church will adopt 500 children in three years.

Individual ministries abound, like Orphan's Ransom, which helps evangelicals pay international adoption fees that can range from $20,000 to $63,000. Churches report a "contagious" "adoption culture" in which even small congregations have adopted dozens of children in just a few years. Movement leaders say this viral effect is key to building the movement. "Get as many people in the church to adopt, and adopt as many kids as you can," said one speaker at the 2010 Adopting for Life Conference, noting the particular power of a pastor's example. Following that advice, in June [2011] the SBC [Southern Baptist Convention], joined with Bethany Christian Services to begin subsidizing Southern Baptist pastors' adoption costs.

Observers from adoption lobby groups mention two watershed moments for the movement: Warren's entrance into the orphan care field in 2005 and President Bush's decision in 2008 to name Jedd Medefind, a former Republican staffer in the California legislature, as head of the White House Office of Faith-Based and Community Initiatives. Medefind is now the affable president of Christian Alliance for Orphans, a coalition of eighty Christian groups, and Warren's church is helping to set up an adoption program in Rwanda.

"It was kind of a perfect storm," reflects Tom DiFilipo, president of the Joint Council on International Children's Services (JCICS), an influential secular adoption advocacy group that has sought to partner with the evangelical movement. "We hit that moment when a movement really starts to ramp up and get the attention of the public." ...

For many adoption reformers, the Silsby affair changed the script for how adoption is discussed. Karen Moline, a board member of the watchdog group Parents for Ethical Adoption Reform, says Silsby "put a face to the worst part of what international adoption can be, which is entitlement," meaning American parents' sense of entitlement to developing nations' children.

An Inaccurate Picture of the "Orphan Crisis"

Susie Krabacher, an American and devout Christian, is director of Mercy and Sharing, a Haitian orphanage founded in

1994 to care for severely disabled, abandoned children, which does not perform adoptions. She says there is enormous economic pressure on Haitian parents to relinquish children. Many orphanages in Haiti provide for children whose parents can't afford to feed them but who remain involved and visit often. But Haiti also has a history of unethical adoption programs. Post-earthquake, Krabacher says, they have become "the biggest money-making operation in Haiti." Indeed, many orphanages, mindful of high international adoption fees, tell struggling parents that they should give up one of their children. The financial desperation in Haiti is so intense and the coercion so pervasive, Krabacher says, that the vast majority of Mercy and Sharing's 181 employees "would have to look at the option of giving up a child if they didn't have a job."

This gets at the central problem in how most evangelical adoption ministries define the scope of the worldwide "orphan crisis." As with the misleading estimates of Haitian orphans, the global numbers most frequently mentioned—ranging from 132 million to 210 million—paint an inaccurate picture, willfully misconstruing UNICEF tallies of developing nations' vulnerable children, a category that includes children who have lost only one parent or who live with extended family.

Susan Bissell, UNICEF's chief of child protection, says no good estimate exists of the number of orphans worldwide, but a 2004 UNICEF report calculated that there were at least 16 million children worldwide who had lost both parents.

"There are not 145 million kids out there waiting for someone in America to adopt them," says Paul Myhill, president of the evangelical orphan ministry World Orphans, which he calls a "black sheep" in his field for its prioritization of in-country orphan care over adoption. "It's unfair to bat these statistics around without using all the qualifiers."

But those numbers have their effect. In July [2011], Bethany Christian Services announced that 'three of the largest

Christian-based adoption agencies,' including itself, were "seeing record numbers of adoptions." Bethany attributes the increase to the evangelical adoption movement as well as the crisis in Haiti, which inspired nearly 20,000 inquiries from across the United States, even though Haiti, post-quake, was quickly closed for new adoptions. Agencies like Bethany explained that they easily redirected this outpouring of enthusiasm to more open markets, like Ethiopia.

The problem is that Ethiopia, which last year [2010] was poised to become the world's top "sending country," is beset by numerous ethical scandals. In 2009 and 2010 investigations by the Australian Broadcasting Corporation and CBS News found evidence that Christian World Adoption [CWA]—a US agency whose slogan is "God is in control of our agency and your adoption"—had recruited and allegedly even bought children from intact families, some of whom didn't understand the permanency of adoption. (CWA claimed that these cases were misunderstandings and charged that it was being persecuted for its Christian beliefs.) In January [2011] the State Department hosted a conference call to discuss ethical difficulties surrounding Ethiopia's adoption program. Just weeks later came the announcement that the license for Minnesota-based Christian agency Better Future Adoption Services had been revoked by the Ethiopian government over accusations of child trafficking. And in March [2011], Ethiopia's government announced it was cutting the rate of new adoptions by 90 percent.

Just after the Haiti earthquake, the Christian Alliance for Orphans advertised that its sixth-annual summit would produce a "long-term response" for Haiti's orphans. By late April 2010, when nearly 1,200 Christians gathered for the summit at a megachurch outside Minneapolis, organizers had to contend with the shadow Silsby had cast. Even Moore worried that the scandal would "give a black eye to the orphan-care movement."

L.W. Nixon Library
Butler Community College
901 South Haverhill Road
El Dorado, Kansas 67042-3280

Bending the Rules to Save Children

"We're killing ourselves with these ethical lapses," says Chuck Johnson, president of the secular adoption lobby group the National Council for Adoption (NCFA). "I think Christians are the worst at this sometimes, about the ends justifying the means. 'I will do anything to save this one child's life'; 'I will falsify a visa application if I have to.'"

[T]he Haiti earthquake helped accelerate the rise of the evangelical adoption movement, and increased its influence.

In early 2010, Johnson told me, NCFA held an online ethics seminar that drew roughly twenty-five representatives from religious and secular adoption agencies. As part of the webinar, NCFA took a blind poll of participants' responses to various ethical situations. Either through ignorance or a willingness to bend the rules, 20–30 percent of agency representatives gave answers that were tantamount to committing visa fraud or other serious violations. "You'll hear people saying, I'm following God's law, not man's laws," Johnson says.

Brian Luwis, founder of the evangelical agency America World Adoption and a Christian Alliance board member, says ardent adoptive parents can wreak havoc for those coming after them. "I call them 'adoption crazies,'" he says. "They're such strong advocates, they'll do things in desperation to have a child they think is theirs. Some are really unlawful, falsifying an adoption or something like that. Many won't get caught, but once you get caught, what have you done to the system?" It's not hard to imagine how movement rhetoric that casts international adoption as emergency rescue and spiritual battle could inspire a willingness to use any means necessary. . . .

Despite the Silsby affair, the Haiti earthquake helped accelerate the rise of the evangelical adoption movement, and increased its influence. At the Christian Alliance summit, JCICS's

[Joint Council on International Children' Services] DiFilipo implored the audience to advocate for less restrictive adoption policies, pointing to the drop in international adoptions from nearly 23,000 in 2004 to a projected 7,000 by 2012.

These numbers underlie a feeling among adoption advocates that even though demand is increasing, International adoption is under siege. "The days of a large sending country are over," Johnson has said.

The decrease is often attributed to the closure of Guatemala and the slowdown in China. DiFilipo says the threat is far broader, with eight or nine countries "functionally suspending" intercountry adoption within the past three years—something he attributes to "institutional bias" against international adoption rather than documented ethical lapses. . . .

[E]vangelical advocates admit that the system is troubled, but they insist that expanding international adoption is necessary. . . .

Juntunen of Both Ends Burning believes the chokepoint created as newly mobilized evangelicals enter the tightening adoption market will spark outrage that will transform the system—cutting red tape, and possibly needed safeguards, along the way. "We've created this culture of adoption, and now more and more people want to participate and are left frustrated because they're denied the opportunity to pursue what they want to pursue," Juntunen told me. "Well, that's where social movements happen. I think that this culture of adoption will be the force, the catalyst, for change."

And the pressure won't be coming just from evangelicals. In June [2011], Together for Adoption and other evangelical leaders will meet with Juntunen and his network of secular adoption advocates to discuss ways to reverse the international adoption freefall.

After a year of headlines concerning improperly adopted children, from Haiti to Nepal to Ethiopia, evangelical advocates admit that the system is troubled, but they insist that expanding international adoption is necessary and, if done right, beautiful. "There's always going to need to be tremendous vigilance that compassionate intentions lead to compassionate outcomes," says the Christian Alliance's [Jedd] Medefind. "But if you're not willing to deal with complexity, it would be wise to stay away from efforts to address the world's needs."

Despite the altruistic motives of many evangelical adopters, the size and wealth of their movement is likely to tip the balance of a system that already responds too blithely to the moral and humanitarian concerns raised by poor countries and all too readily to Western demand.

4

Citizenship Should Be Granted to Foreign-Born Adoptees of US Citizens

Joseph D'Agostino

Joseph D'Agostino was an advocacy journalist in Washington, D.C., and received his Juris Doctor degree from the University of Virginia School of Law in 2012.

Many American citizens adopt children from other countries, and the US government recognizes these adoptions to be legal. But often unbeknownst to the parents or the adopted children, a legal adoption does not always guarantee US citizenship for the adoptees. Because of confusing visa laws that can easily be misinterpreted, foreign-born adopted children can be classified as legal permanent residents (LPRs) instead of citizens. As a result, adoptees may be denied the right to obtain a passport and to vote, and can even be deported to an unfamiliar country for committing a minor offense. A system that denies citizenship to legally adopted foreign-born children violates human rights principles; automatic citizenship should be granted to all such children.

Adoption is a legal means to provide families who have adopted with the same rights as biological families. Under American law, children who have been adopted are expected to have the same rights as biological children, and that goal of equality is also reflected in legal and social standards of inter-

Joseph D'Agostino, "Equalizing the Treatment of Foreign-Born Adopted Children," *Adoption Advocate*, March 2011. Copyright © 2011 by National Council for Adoption. All rights reserved. Adapted by permission.

national human rights conventions. Yet for thousands of internationally-born children legally adopted as minors by American couples, that promise of equality under the law is violated in one of the most fundamental ways possible, both today and historically.

An Incorrect Assumption of U.S. Citizenship

Many children legally adopted from overseas by American citizens and raised in the United States do not receive automatic American citizenship, and often both the children and their adoptive parents are unaware of this fact. The lack of citizenship becomes an issue when the adoptive parent, or the adopted person as an adult, applies for a passport, tries to vote, attempts to obtain instate tuition at a college, or otherwise runs into a situation in which citizenship must be proven. Then they are denied the rights and privileges that Americans take for granted. They can even face mandatory deportation to countries they cannot remember for minor, first-time offenses. For example, one woman, adopted at birth by American citizens, was in the process of applying for citizenship and was told she would be deported back to her country of birth because she had pulled another woman's hair many years before. . . .

[A]dopted children should be guaranteed rights identical to those of biological children.

The problem lies in an all too familiar interaction of laws that did not work entirely as intended and a bureaucracy that does not know quite what to do with those laws. The result is children who are legally adopted by American citizens and raised here, but who never become citizens, often without knowing that they are not citizens. Even knowing that they are not citizens sometimes doesn't help. "We're told to go in one direction and when we do, we're told to switch gears and go into another direction," said Scott Mulvihill. "And when we look for counsel from the government to give us a definite answer, we get stuck with people who are supposed to be working on marriage contracts rather than immigration contracts."

McLane Layton has an intimate knowledge of both the law and how it affects families with adopted children. Layton served as Legislative Counsel to Sen. Don Nickles [Oklahoma] from 1990 to 2005. She and her husband also adopted three children from Eastern Europe in 1995. She was shocked to discover that even though the U.S. government fully recognized the adoptions as legal, and both she and her husband were U.S. citizens, "my children were not going to be automatic U.S. citizens." There is a resounding dissonance in the fact that individuals can be recognized as the children of American citizens without being recognized as American citizens themselves. It is a situation most Americans probably think is legally impossible.

This is a tear in the fabric of the rights adoption is intended to afford: adopted children should be guaranteed rights identical to those of biological children. "I was offended every time I had to sit down to fill out forms to naturalize my children. My husband and I are U.S. citizens and had I given birth to my children overseas they would be citizens. Adopted children are supposed to be treated the same as biological children under U.S. law, but in this instance they are not," says Layton.

Confusing and Misunderstood Laws

Mrs. Layton shared her concerns with Sen. Nickles, and the eventual result was the Child Citizenship Act (CCA), passed in 2000. "On February 27, 2001, more than 100,000 foreignborn adopted children across the nation were given the wonderful gift of American citizenship as a result of enactment of the Child Citizenship Act of 2000," says Layton's education and advocacy group, Equality for Adopted Children (EACH). "The CCA amended the Immigration and Nationality Act to confer United States citizenship automatically on certain foreign-born children adopted by citizens of the United States."

[T]he system should be streamlined in the interests of clarity, convenience, and the best interests of the children. . . .

Unfortunately, the CCA . . . did not work entirely as intended. The U.S. State Department interpreted the statute to make a distinction between foreign-born children who enter the United States on IR-3 and IH-3 visas and those who enter on IR-4 and IH-4 visas. Those who enter on IR-3 and IH-3 visas have been seen and accepted by both adoptive parents, and they automatically receive citizenship upon entering the United States. Those who enter on IR-4 and IH-4 visas, who have a final adoption, but may have met only one or neither adoptive parent, do not receive citizenship automatically.

Why did the Department of State adopt this interpretation? "I've not received a good answer on that," says Layton. It may be, she said, that there was a fear that parents who had not yet met a child would reject him or her, creating a situation in which a foreign-born child that might be rejected by his or her adoptive American family could become an American citizen. Yet, later rejected or not, children who enter the United States on IR-4 or IH-4 visas with final adoption decrees are already legally the children of the adopting Americans. Layton believes the system should be streamlined in the interests of clarity, convenience, and the best interests of the children: those children who enter on IR-4 or IH-4 visas and who are legally adopted by American citizens before coming to the United States should receive citizenship automatically upon arrival here, just like children who are adopted and enter on IR-3 and IH-3 visas. Instead, they become legal permanent residents (LPRs).

Though no precise statistics are available, advocate and author Jean Erichsen estimates that "given that approximately 300,000 children have been adopted internationally by American parents over the past thirty years, the number could well be in the thousands." Further, the number continues to grow as approximately half of the children adopted internationally enter the United States on IR-4 or IH-4 visas. Not only has the Department of State's treatment of children entering the United States on IR-4 or IH-4 visas created a continually growing class of adopted children who do not receive automatic citizenship upon entry, the CCA did not apply to anyone age eighteen or over at the time of its enactment. Thus, there are two distinct groups living in this country in citizenship limbo, often without their or their adoptive parents' knowledge. "People assume that the children they adopt receive citizenship, and adopted children probably don't even think about the question at all, even when they grow up," says Layton.

Then something happens to make them think about it, Layton says. "Adult adoptees sometimes find out they are not citizens when they apply for passports, apply to college, enlist in the military, or when they are charged with a minor offense and can be subjected to deportation," she says. By the time parents of adopted children or adult adoptees figure out that they must apply for citizenship, even though their adoptions were legal, it is often too late. "Documents are lost or cannot be obtained from the developing countries where they originated," she says. Even the best-informed parents can face challenges. Though the Laytons adopted three siblings in 1995, they still face concerns to this day. "We have only one certified copy of their birth certificates from their birth country and we can't easily get more," she said. "Do you know how often people are asked for certified copies of their birth certificates? I can't get certified copies for my children from my own state unless I re-adopt them in my state, although re-adoption is not required by my state," Layton says.

The Beginning of the Problem

Though the current anomaly of some legally adopted children not receiving citizenship automatically is long-standing, it rarely created a problem until 1996. The Antiterrorism and Effective Death Penalty Act (AEDPA) of 1996 and the Illegal Immigration Reform and Immigrant Responsibility Act (IIRIRA) of 1996 increased the numbers of LPRs eligible for mandatory deportation. Under these laws, deportation has become far more likely, because the acts that require deportation were expanded and that could be applied both retroactively and for minor crimes that were not subject to deportation at the time of conviction. Under AEDPA, crimes for which a sentence of one year or longer could be imposed often became grounds for the mandatory deportation of those convicted. Formerly a much more restrictive category, "aggravated felony" was used for the purpose of mandatory deportation, however this category was expanded to include such non-violent offenses as document fraud, illegal gambling, prostitution, and other offenses.

The current system of denying American citizenship to some foreign-born children legally adopted by American citizens from overseas seems to violate widely accepted principles embodied in international human rights statements.

IIRIRA further expanded the meaning of "aggravated felony." A conviction of one year instead of the previous five year requirement now triggers mandatory deportation for crimes of theft or crimes of violence. The money laundering threshold went from $100,000 to $10,000. Many new offenses were added that could trigger deportation and the threshold length of possible prison terms reduced greatly. It's also important to note that the prison terms did not have to be actually imposed upon an individual, they only needed to be within the sentencing limits that a judge could impose. The number of LPRs subject to deportation increased dramatically and included some of those adopted by American citizens as infants and who had no familial, linguistic, or cultural ties to the countries of their birth, many for non-violent acts and often without any knowledge that there was a risk of deportation. Even felony DWIs [driving while intoxicated] have been found to trigger mandatory deportation.

Mary Anne Gehris, adopted by American citizens from Germany as an infant, applied for citizenship in 1997 and when she received a letter from INS in 1999, she expected it to be a date to be sworn in as a citizen. Instead it was a notice that she was to be deported. The charge that triggered her deportation was an eleven-year-old misdemeanor for pulling the hair of another woman while fighting over a boyfriend. The charge had been suspended with a year's probation, meaning the judge at the time expected nothing of her but a year of good behavior. However, because it was possible to be charged for up to a year of jail time for this offense, it was considered an aggravated felony under IIRIRA. The state of Georgia saved Mary Ann Gehris by pardoning this minimal charge so she would not be deported. Many others are deported for similar minimal acts.

Violation of Human Rights Ideals

The current system of denying American citizenship to some foreign-born children legally adopted by American citizens from overseas seems to violate widely accepted principles embodied in international human rights statements. For example, the 1986 UN Declaration on the Social and Legal Principles Relating to the Protection and the Welfare of Children, approved by the General Assembly, states, "The child should at all times have a name, a nationality and a legal representative. The child should not, as a result of foster placement, adoption or any alternative regime, be deprived of his or her name, nationality or legal representative unless the child thereby acquires a new name, nationality or legal representative." Arguably, by removing a child from his birth country and causing the resulting loss of cultural and other connections to that country, including a de facto loss of the protections of that country's laws, without granting him or her the nationality of the new country of permanent residence, American law is in violation of this article.

Further, Article 22 states, "No intercountry adoption should be considered before it has been established that the child is legally free for adoption and that any pertinent documents necessary to complete the adoption, such as the consent of competent authorities, will become available. It must also be established that the child will be able to migrate and to join the prospective adoptive parents and may obtain their nationality." Though it is true that children adopted from overseas can obtain American citizenship if their adoptive parents are aware of the need for further bureaucratic measures after legal adoption and then pursue those measures with the vigor and money needed, the reality is that this ideal is not being followed. For the average American adoptive parent, managing all the details of the many forms of identification is burdensome because of the time and money it takes to do this for the varied forms of identification, from passports to Social Security cards.

The UN Convention on the Rights of the Child says, "Ensure that the child concerned by inter-country adoption enjoys safeguards and standards equivalent to those existing in the case of national adoption . . ." This passage does not address nationality directly, but children adopted within the United States keep their nationality and enjoy the safeguards of being nationals of the country in which they permanently reside. Some internationally adopted children receive different, lesser treatment.

Chuck Johnson, President and CEO of the National Council For Adoption, is cautiously optimistic that a piece of legislation that would clarify the CCA to grant automatic citizenship to all foreign-born children adopted by American citizens will go forward this session [2011] with broad bipartisan support as the CCA did in 2000. It will bear similarities to a section of previously proposed legislation on this issue, the Foreign Adopted Children Equality Act (FACE). Advocates hope that the new legislation will accomplish what the CCA was intended to, providing automatic U.S. citizenship to all foreign-adopted children of American citizens upon their arrival in the U.S.

A statutory fix is necessary, Layton says. "I think that deporting the legally adopted child of an American citizen to a foreign country is unconscionable and unconstitutional. Until legislation makes it undeniably clear that foreignadopted children of American citizens are American citizens, just like biological children born abroad to American citizens, inequities will continue to exist."

5

Ethnic Identity Is Important in Transracial Adoptions

Nicole M. Callahan

Nicole M. Callahan, a graduate of Johns Hopkins University and a Korean American transracial adoptee, is director of publications at the National Council for Adoption, an adoption advocacy organization. Callahan is also the editor of the organization's publication Adoption Advocate *and has written numerous articles, policy papers, and legislative testimony on a wide range of adoption issues. The story of Nicole's reunion with her sister can be found in the book* Somebody's Child: Stories About Adoption, *edited by Bruce Gillespie and Lynne Van Luven (TouchWood, 2011).*

The number of multiracial families in America is growing, as is the number of transracial adoptions. Yet for many Americans the subject of race is still difficult to discuss, even between parents and their foreign-born adopted children. Ignoring racial differences, however, can actually harm adopted children of color, making them feel separate from and inferior to other children. Most adoption professionals and child welfare experts believe that ethnic identity and cultural heritage are subjects that need to be discussed openly and honestly with children as well as with friends and other members of the community. In fact, actively socializing with people of diverse racial cultures would help foster self-esteem and lessen any sense of isolation for children of transracial adoption.

Nicole M. Callahan, "Race and Identity in Transracial Adoption: Suggestions for Adoptive Parents," *Adoption Advocate*, August 2011. Copyright © 2011 by National Council for Adoption. All rights reserved. Adapted by permission.

"Growing up as an Asian American adoptee was often like stumbling through a maze blindfolded," says Marijane. "When my parents adopted me, I was automatically [initiated] into a white society, shut off from my birth culture. My parents did not know how that would impact me growing up."

A Color-Aware Approach—Not a Color-Blind Approach

Some white prospective adoptive parents might question their ability to parent children of color, while others may underestimate or prematurely dismiss potential issues and challenges. Most adoption professionals and child welfare experts agree that parents should not adopt across racial lines unless they are prepared to—at minimum—help their child learn about her racial identity and cultural heritage, help her find and encourage quality relationships with individuals who share her heritage, acknowledge the continued existence of racial prejudice and help her learn to confront and cope with it, and assist her in developing a positive, mature, and healthy self-image (which will, by necessity, include her racial and cultural identity). None of this is possible without entering into *a realistic and ongoing discussion of race,* both the child's and that of others, and dealing with any questions and issues that arise in a thoughtful and age-appropriate way.

[P]rospective adoptive parents who are considering a transracial adoption cannot afford to ignore the issue of race or explore it only superficially.

Yet talking about race in America can prove difficult for people of *all* races—for people of color who lack safe, nonjudgmental spaces to share their experiences honestly and without fear of prejudice or misunderstanding; and for white people who may sometimes feel attacked when others discuss the continued existence of ignorance, racism, and white privilege in our country. Many white Americans, including some prospective adoptive parents, shy away from frank and open discussions about race; some even claim that such discussions are unnecessary. It is easy to understand their apprehension. Some may be afraid of giving offense, or worried that even mentioning someone's race might provoke anger or suspicion. They may be of the opinion that America has overcome its long history of racial prejudice, and that only the most blatant, intentional, and obviously offensive instances of racism are worthy of the name. They may believe that good people with good intentions cannot harbor racist thoughts or prejudices. Or they may simply hope that, by ignoring race entirely and taking a so-called "colorblind" approach, they can keep prejudice and racism from harming their children and their families.

However, prospective adoptive parents who are considering a transracial adoption cannot afford to ignore the issue of race or explore it only superficially. When it comes to adoption, and in particular transracial and transcultural adoption, love and good intentions are not enough. Parents must be their child's first and strongest allies when facing every difficulty or challenge that may arise—including those resulting from prejudice, racial stereotypes, and the still fraught state of race relations in our society. Adoptive parents must also be prepared to educate others and advocate for their children even within their own families and networks of friends.

"For white parents, it's essential to become comfortable thinking and talking about race," says Dr. Betsy Vonk, PhD. a professor and director of the MSW [Masters Degree in Social Work] program at the University of Georgia, and the adoptive mother of two daughters from China. "You have to start while the kids are young—that way, both the parents and children will have a chance to get used to thinking and talking about race before the teasing and the really tough discussions begin." . . .

The View from a Transracial Adoptee's Perspective

The moment you adopt across racial lines, your family is a multiracial, multicultural one. And when it comes to transracial adoption and multiracial family life, unfortunately, not all communities in America are created equal. Thanks to both adoption and interracial unions, the number of multiracial families in America is growing exponentially, but there are plenty of communities and towns in which such families are still few and far between.

> [T]he isolation felt by many transracial adoptees . . . could overwhelm the natural interest and curiosity they might feel.

Before adopting a child of color, take a close look at your town, your current neighborhood, your school options, your social activities, your religious community, etc. Try and view all of these through the eyes of a nonwhite child. This proves difficult for some prospective adoptive parents; for many members of the majority, "diversity" within their communities may be viewed as something "nice" or even desirable, but not necessarily very important. White people living in the U.S. who reside in mostly white neighborhoods, work and/or socialize almost exclusively with other white people, send their children to predominantly white schools, and live in mostly white communities, may never have had cause to examine or question the lack of racial or cultural diversity among the people with whom they regularly associate. They may well be comfortable with the status quo, and that is understandable. But when white parents intend to adopt a child of color, it is their responsibility to look at their communities, organizations, activities, and even their primary social relationships through the eyes of that child.

How comfortable will your child feel as a member of a minority group in your area? Would your child be the only person of color in her school? At your church? On your street? Would she regularly see many faces that looked at all like hers? Can these places and people help provide her with an environment in which she could be comfortable, easily find friends, feel confident and thrive?

If not, it is a problem. Not necessarily an insurmountable one, but one requiring some changes—including some that may seem radical at first. You may feel strongly called to adopt across racial lines, but if you primarily live and move and socialize in a community in which your adopted child would be one of only a handful of minorities—perhaps the only one from a particular group—then transracial adoption may require you to make some changes first. . . .

It is important for parents to make it clear that they support and want to be a part of their child's cultural exploration. The child may also be more interested if his family lives in a diverse community where he can see that his culture is represented, and if his family also fosters relationships with individuals who share that culture. Otherwise, the isolation felt by many transracial adoptees, the sense of being different from family and friends, could overwhelm the natural interest and curiosity they might feel. Many transracial adoptees that live in primarily white communities spend their childhood and adolescence simply wanting to "blend in," and these feelings are not very conducive to meaningful exploration of their cultures and countries of origin.

"[My parents] did not talk about my birth heritage nor encourage me to investigate, but rather minimized my ethnicity due to this lack of awareness," says transracial adoptee Marijane. "For many years, I downplayed it and tried to fit into the 'whiteness' all around me, never quite feeling like I was good enough, or that I fit into the social norm."

Fostering a Strong Sense of Self

A great deal can depend on whether the adopted child perceives that her parents are open to and comfortable with her curiosity and exploration. Children, especially young children, will naturally take their lead from their parents. If they sense that their parents do not wish to draw attention to or discuss their racial identity, their cultural heritage, or their country of origin, they may shy away from raising these issues themselves—or else wait until they are able to explore them without their parents' participation or encouragement. This is why many transracial adoptees report never learning about their heritage until adulthood—meaning that they lost years of opportunity, years during which they had a decreased understanding of who they were and where they came from. . . .

"Those who plan to adopt a child or children from another country *must* help their child develop an appropriate sense of cultural and racial identity, which further increases their chances of developing a strong sense of self," says Marijane. "It is the adoptive parents' responsibility to ensure that their child is given opportunities to learn about his or her birth culture beginning at an early age. Otherwise, an injustice is imposed on the children of transracial adoption, whether they are aware of it or not." . . .

It is especially important to provide transracially adopted children with the opportunity to cultivate relationships with individuals who share their racial and cultural background . . .

Of course ignorance of the challenges, experiences, and lives of people of color can harm white children as well; it can cause them to embrace stereotypes, fear differences, or perpetuate inherited, ingrained prejudices simply because they never had the opportunity to know better. But such ignorance can be especially harmful to adopted children of color, who must then work out their own racial identities without recourse to family members, friends, or trusted mentors who share it.

It is especially important to provide transracially adopted children with the opportunity to cultivate relationships with individuals who share their racial and cultural background—to help them understand and appreciate their origins and history, to give them more allies, and to provide them with greater support as they navigate a racially diverse, but still prejudiced society. . . .

Given its potential and unique challenges, it is understandable that some parents may feel daunted by or ill equipped to pursue a transracial adoption. Just like adoption itself, it is not for every parent or every family. But while transracial adoption does raise a set of issues not found in same-race adoptions, it can bring its own joys and rewards as well. Through transracial adoption, many children find loving families of their own, and their parents, extended family members, and friends have the opportunity to witness, learn about, and better understand the history and experiences of people of color.

Parents of transracially adopted children must work diligently to practice *empathy*—to make it their business to know about the experiences of their children as young people of color, foster the positive development of their self-image and identity, and share in their hurts and triumphs, joys and sufferings. It is very possible for open and thoughtful parents to create healthy, happy, well-adjusted, culturally rich, and emotionally whole multiracial families through transracial adoption. Like any other type of adoption, a successful and mutually fulfilling transracial adoption requires a great deal of time, trial, and effort on the part of families, but the benefits—for both children and parents—make the challenges more than worthwhile.

6

Ethnic Identity Should Not Be Paramount in Transracial Adoptions

Jeneen Interlandi

Jeneen Interlandi is a reporter for Newsweek *magazine.*

Many American adoptive parents, unable to conceive but desperately wanting a family, are turning to other countries to adopt babies. Critics of such international adoptions argue that the adopted children will suffer from a fractured sense of self and a loss of ethnic identity. Studies have shown, however, that transracial adoptees have no higher risk of psychological problems than same-race adoptees. Furthermore, while many adoptive parents do make an effort to instill a sense of cultural heritage in their children, the most important considerations should be the welfare of the children and the opportunities afforded them in a loving, responsible family.

Earthquakes in Haiti and Chile have left thousands of children orphaned and revived debates over the value of international adoption. In the weeks since a group of American missionaries were arrested [in 2010] on charges of child-trafficking, Haiti's orphans have continued to trickle across her borders. More than 300 Haitian children have been adopted by families in France, and the State Department estimates that nearly 2,000 will have been placed with U.S. families by month's end [in March, 2010]. Thanks to enhanced

Jeneen Interlandi, "The Case for International Adoption," *Newsweek*, March 1, 2010.
Copyright © 2010 Newsweek, Inc. All rights reserved. Reprinted by permission.

scrutiny by both Haitian and U.S. officials in the wake of the missionary debacle, it appears that the vast majority of those adoptions will be of legitimate orphans and not child-trafficking victims.

That won't silence critics, who argue that taking orphaned children from their birth countries and raising them elsewhere robs those nations of their most valuable resource and leaves the adoptees with a hopelessly fractured ethnic identity, only to satisfy the capricious whims of wealthy Westerners. (The contentious term cultural genocide is sometimes employed.) Opponents of international adoption routinely point to the abundance of orphans here in the U.S. where they claim it is both easier and cheaper to adopt. From there, they typically question the motives of "eager white Americans" who would endeavor "to adopt children that look nothing like them,"—as if every would-be parent who sought to adopt overseas were somehow trying to be [actress] Angelina Jolie. There are some persistent myths behind that argument that need dispelling. But first, a quick story:

International Adoptees Are Afforded Newfound Opportunities

My own parents suffered through a string of miscarriages and failed attempts to adopt in the U.S. before fetching my older sister, twin brother, and me from a dilapidated orphanage in Medellín, Colombia. It was the late 1970s, and we were infants—two of us premature and very sick. They nursed us back to health, brought us to a working-class suburb of New Jersey and promptly went about the business of raising us. Among the many things they took pains to instill (like work ethic, faith in God, and a healthy appreciation for good lasagna), a sense of Colombian-ness was not included. Nor was it to be acquired elsewhere: together my siblings and I made up about half the town's Colombian population.

But if we lacked a clear blueprint for our ethnic identities, we still had plenty of other parameters from which to forge our sense of selves: we were blue-collar kids from Jersey. We grew up amongst the mostly Irish- and Italian-American children of nurses, plumbers, and store clerks. Like them, we indulged in all the rituals of our particular American upbringing. And like most internationally adopted children, we turned out just fine.

My loss of ethnic heritage has been more than compensated for in the multitude of opportunities afforded by my adoption.

To be sure, there are some significant and seemingly unclosable gaps in our cultural identities. I remember eagerly befriending two Colombian kids that moved to our town in junior high, only to find out that we had nothing special in common. "I'm Colombian too," I exclaimed to one of them, a girl the same age as me. She smiled and started speaking in Spanish. I furrowed my brow to show that I didn't understand. "Where are you from?" she asked in English. "Medellín," I said. "No," she said, laughing. "You definitely aren't."

In later years my twin brother (who is darker than my sister and me) would occasionally be subject to racial profiling. And, as we belatedly discovered, all three of us would have to go through the complicated and lengthy process of naturalization before we could obtain driver's licenses (or register to vote or apply for financial aid for college). We were immigrants and minorities—but only sometimes. The same was true of our Italian experience. I know more about Palermo and my father's upbringing in 1950s Bensonhurst than I ever will about Medellín, but I feel as dishonest calling myself Italian or Italian-American as I do calling myself Colombian. That's OK by me. My loss of ethnic heritage has been more than compensated for in the multitude of opportunities afforded by my adoption. Besides, I kind of like being a cultural chameleon (Colombian by birth, Sicilian by adoption, and American by upbringing). It makes me unique.

I won't pretend my experience is the same as it would be if I were black or Asian, or even a darker shade of Hispanic, and I'm not trying to say that race doesn't matter at all. But race and ethnicity shouldn't be the foremost concerns of adoptive parents, foreign governments, or society at large. The primary consideration should be the welfare of the children in question. Where will they have the best chance at happy, fulfilling lives? How best can the global community ensure their health and safety?

[I]t is patently false that the high-profile choices of a few celebrities have triggered an international adoption boom.

Motivations of Adoptive Parents

Within the U.S., the federal government has long since determined that while race and ethnicity merit consideration, they should not be the deciding factors in any adoption. That's because numerous studies show that transracial and transcultural adoptees don't face any higher risks of psychological problems or identity issues than domestic, same-ethnicity adoptees. As uncomfortable as it makes some people to acknowledge, white parents are capable of raising emotionally healthy black, Asian, and Hispanic children. And that's no less true when the child comes from another country.

Those who argue that prospective parents should "just adopt in the U.S." don't understand the motivations of most adoptive parents. If would-be adopters were acting out of some profound sense of charity, then reasonable people could debate the merits of alleviating greater suffering abroad vs. considerably less suffering closer to home. (In Colombia in

1977, children who weren't adopted by the age of 9 or 10 were turned out onto the street: girls mostly became prostitutes, boys joined the guerrilla armies or found work in the coca fields. By contrast, American orphans of the same generation were guaranteed food, shelter, and some form of education until they turned 18.)

But the fact is, most adoptive parents are like mine: they are unable to conceive but desperately want to experience parenthood—in all its permutations. That means they want babies. In the U.S., 60 percent of eligible orphans are more than 5 years old. Several critics have argued that the supply of Third-World infants is not a natural occurrence but a response to the demand of adoption markets in the West. This is only partly true: yes, Western demand motivates child-traffickers. But even after child trafficking is taken out of the equation, there are still many more infants to adopt abroad than there are in the U.S. (6.6 million compared with less than 60,000, based on an analysis of data from Unicef [United Nations Children's Fund] and the United States Department of Health and Human Services). International adoption is expensive (up to $40,000 in many cases) and takes a long time (one to three years on average)—long enough to consider all of the challenges and complexities that raising a child of different cultural or ethnic heritage will entail. It's not a process one enters into lightly.

In fact, most parents choose international adoption only after being repeatedly stymied by U.S. adoption protocols—from birth parents that change their minds at the last minute, to stringent and sometimes arbitrary requirements on the part of domestic adoption agencies. Speaking of which, it is patently false that the high-profile choices of a few celebrities have triggered an international adoption boom. In fact, in the U.S. especially, international adoption rates have plummeted—from about 25,000 in 2004 to less than 13,000 in 2009. Today, they are at an all time low, thanks to the greater availability of contraception, a global crackdown on child-trafficking, and better economic conditions in places like Russia and China, the birthplace of many internationally adopted orphans.

The Welfare of the Child Is Paramount

These days, internationally adoptive parents often go to great lengths to preserve their adoptive children's sense of cultural heritage—a big change since I was adopted from Colombia. According to one Harvard survey, 15 percent of transracially adoptive parents move to more ethnically diverse neighborhoods after adopting, to enhance their child's exposure to other people of the same ethnicity. Many parents take corresponding language and cooking lessons and many more immerse themselves in the diaspora communities of their children's birth countries. Some also participate, with their children, in "homeland tours" offered by international adoption agencies.

At the same time, adult adoptees from Korea, China, and elsewhere have formed national organizations to facilitate homeland visits and lobby for dual citizenship, among other things. There is no reason to think that Haitian orphans won't do the same. To be sure, they will face barriers to forging coherent racial and ethnic identities—almost all internationally and interracially adopted children do. But those barriers won't be insurmountable and they won't necessarily be devastating. In the end, what matters most is not where a child is from, but whether or not that child is well loved and well cared for by a responsible family—regardless of race or nationality.

7

Transracial Adoptions from Foster Care Pose Unique Challenges

Susan Smith, Ruth McRoy, Madelyn Freundlich, and Joe Kroll

Susan Smith, program and project director of the Evan B. Donaldson Adoption Institute, is also co-director of the Center for Adoption Studies at Illinois State University; Ruth McRoy is the director of the Center for Social Work Research at the University of Texas at Austin; Madelyn Freundlich, the executive director of the Evan B. Donaldson Adoption Institute, is a social worker and lawyer whose work has focused on child welfare policy and practice; and Joe Kroll is the executive director of the North American Council on Adoptable Children.

Studies have shown that children adopted from foster care face a higher risk of behavioral difficulties than do children in the general population. And transracial adoption from foster care introduces additional risk factors, further complicating the adoptee's parent-child relationship, social adjustment, and racial identity. Research suggests, however, that if adoptive parents educate and prepare themselves for the unique issues and challenges inherent in transracial adoptions and foster children, everyone involved—especially the children—will be better served.

Susan Smith, Ruth McRoy, Madelyn Freundlich, and Joe Kroll, "Finding Families for African American Children: The Role of Race & Law in Adoption from Foster Care," Evan B. Donaldson Adoption Institute, May 2008. www.adoptioninstitute.org. Copyright © 2008 by Evan B. Donaldson Adoption Institute. All rights reserved. Reproduced by permission.

Just like their counterparts in birth families, children in adoptive families have their own unique combinations of potential and risk; likewise, parents of all sorts bring to the formation of families their own constellations of strengths and limitations. Adoption itself infuses issues into family life for everyone involved, such as loss and identity. And transracial adoption adds yet another layer of complexity. The current body of research supports three key conclusions:

1. Transracial adoption in itself does not produce psychological or social maladjustment problems in children.

2. Transracially adopted children and their families face a range of challenges, and the manner in which parents handle them facilitates or hinders children's development.

3. Children in foster care come to adoption with many risk factors that pose challenges for healthy development. For these children, research points to the importance of adoptive placements with families who can address their individual issues and maximize their opportunity to develop to their fullest potential.

Transracial Adoptive Parents Need Preparation and Education

Specifically, research suggests that children in transracial adoptions can confront important challenges—and these are important issues to consider and address in the adoption of African American children from foster care. Parents can support children in successfully addressing these challenges, but they often need preparation and education to understand the issues and strategies for facilitating a positive racial identity. . . .

Adoptive parents who are committed to addressing racial differences and identity issues of transracially adopted children can raise them to be emotionally well-adjusted and culturally competent individuals, but this requires an awareness of the importance of race/ethnicity and the realities of racism, and a commitment to addressing the complexities of these issues with their children throughout their development. Responsible and ethical adoption practice requires preparing parents to understand these issues and to be able to address them with their children. While some adoptive parents will educate themselves, many others will lack sufficient awareness of these issues unless they are prepared by professionals.

Parents . . . often need preparation and education to understand the issues and strategies for facilitating a positive racial identity.

Children from Foster Care Are at Greater Risk for Behavioral Problems

There is a growing body of research on the long-term adjustment of children adopted from foster care. These studies indicate that almost all such children are well-integrated in their new families but, at the same time, are at greater risk of behavior problems than children in the general population or those adopted in infancy who were not in foster care. Studies consistently have found about 40 percent of children adopted from foster care score in the clinical range on standardized measures of behavioral/emotional problems; that is, at the level of children receiving mental health services. Despite these challenges, more than 90 percent of the parents of children adopted from foster care are satisfied with their adoption experience.

Although this body of work provides important information on emotional and behavioral risks for children adopted from foster care in general, little research attention has been given to transracial adoption for this group, making it difficult to reach definitive conclusions. Three studies conducted 15 or more years ago compared outcomes for children transracially and in-racially adopted from foster care. Two focused on disruption, with one finding a higher rate for transracial placements and the other finding no greater disruption risk for such placements.

[T]ransracial adoptive parents were more likely to rate their children as more difficult to raise than were the parents of same-race children.

A study of over 750 families adopting children from the child welfare system by [James Aaron] Rosenthal and [Victor] Groze (1992) found a similar rate of satisfaction among transracial adoptive parents, although outcomes for minority in-racial adoptions were more positive than those in transracial adoptions on many measures. Minority in-racial families reported closer relationships on a standardized parent-child relationship scale than transracial families, and perceptions of support from family and friends were lower among transracial than minority in-racial adoptive families. This study also found that six factors were associated with problematic parent-child relationships among transracial adoptions: adoption by a new family (not foster or kin), older age of child, high family income, behavioral problems, learning disabilities, and the child's dislike of school. The strength of these associations, however, was weaker in White, same-race adoptions and weaker still in minority, same-race adoptions. The authors concluded:

> Stated differently, these factors seem to generate serious problems in transracial placements, moderate problems in white, inracial placements, but only minor problems in minority, inracial placements. . . . Minority, inracial placements were distinguished from the other subgroups by the fact that problems with behavior and in school appear less damaging to the quality of parent-child relationship. . . . In minority, inracial placements, parent-child relationships remain as close with teens as with younger children. This

same pattern was not observed in the other subgroups. The close relationships between teens and adoptive parents in minority, inracial homes suggest that inracial placement may offer distinct advantages for older children ... it is not negative outcomes for transracial placements but instead positive ones for minority, inracial placements that argue convincingly for enhanced recruitment of minority families.

More recently, an Illinois study [conducted in 2003] assessed the adjustment of 1,340 children, ages 6 to 18, adopted from foster care. The study compared transracial and same-race adoptions on several variables. As a measure of overall adjustment, the study used the Behavior Problem Index (BPI), a standardized behavior problem measure listing 28 behavioral problems that is utilized in the National Longitudinal Survey of Youth. The National Survey studied more than 11,500 children and found a mean number of behavior problems of 6.4. In the Illinois study, the mean number of behavior problems for children adopted from foster care was 11.9. African American children had the lowest rates of behavior problems (mean of 10.4 problem behaviors) of all racial/ethnic groups. Important differences were noted, however, between Black children adopted transracially and those adopted by same-race families. The 73 adopted transracially had significantly higher behavior problem scores—a mean of 14.4, compared to 9.9 for the 407 adopted by same-race families. On most other outcomes, such as the parents' closeness to their children or their satisfaction with the adoption, transracially placed children were not significantly different from those adopted in-racially—but transracial adoptive parents were more likely to rate their children as more difficult to raise than were the parents of same-race children.

Foster Care Introduces a "Compounded Developmental Risk"

As previously noted, these findings do not provide sufficient basis for reaching conclusions about the level of problems experienced by Black children in foster care who are adopted transracially compared to those adopted by Black families. The findings, however, indicate the need for further research. Most children adopted from foster care have experienced a constellation of circumstances that pose challenges to their development. The [Jeanne] Howard and [Susan Livingston] Smith study (2003) found Illinois children adopted from foster care had experienced serious neglect (63 percent), prenatal alcohol or drug exposure (60 percent), physical abuse (33 percent), sexual abuse (17 percent), and two or more foster care placements (37 percent). Most had experienced more than one of these risk factors.

When a child's adoptive family is of a different race, it adds another layer of development and adjustment challenges. . . .

The multiple risk factors present in the histories of children in foster care can exponentially complicate their adjustment in new adoptive families. [James] Garbarino's (1992) studies of the impact of high-risk environments on children and the factors associated with resiliency are relevant to these issues. Garabarino uses the term "compounded developmental risk" to capture the cumulative effect of developmental and socio-cultural risk factors in the lives of children in high-risk environments. Although environmental conditions can intensify or mitigate the impact of risk factors, they "often act synergistically, with each compounding the other's effects." Children in foster care who have experienced assaults on their development and well-being require environments that mitigate rather than heighten their vulnerability. They need opportunities to develop nurturing attachments to parents and siblings, succeed in school, establish friendships with other children, and find acceptance and support in all areas of their lives. Garbarino further writes that all children have a "self-righting" tendency by which they strive to overcome past adversities and move on.

Because children adopted from foster care face compounded developmental risk, it is especially important that they achieve permanency with families able to address their needs and maximize their development potential. The negative effects of long-term foster care and aging out of the system have been well documented, further emphasizing the importance of permanent families. When a child's adoptive family is of a different race, it adds another layer of development and adjustment challenges, requiring that families be prepared and supported to meet the child's needs. This is not to say a White family may not offer the best chance for success to a child of color; rather, it underscores the importance of finding a family who can address the child's needs in an optimal manner.

8

Gays and Lesbians Should Be Allowed to Adopt

American Psychological Association

The American Psychological Association (APA), founded in 1892, is a nonprofit scientific and professional organization. Among APA's major purposes is to increase and disseminate knowledge regarding human behavior and to foster the application of psychology to important human concerns, which include human sexuality and familial relationships.

The US Census Bureau reports that hundreds of thousands of gay and lesbian adults are raising children, and according to scientific research, these children are just as psychologically healthy as children raised by heterosexual parents with respect to such issues as self-esteem, behavioral problems, and social relationships. Furthermore, published studies have found that parents' sexual orientation does not affect the sexual orientation of their children. Therefore, gays and lesbians should not be discriminated against in matters of adoption.

A large and growing number of gay men and lesbians raise children, either as single parents or in the context of a committed relationship. Although the exact numbers of lesbian and gay parents in the United States are unknown, [2009] data from the U.S. Census Bureau indicate that, among heads of household who report cohabiting with a same-sex partner,

American Psychological Association, "Amicus Curiae Brief, State of Florida Third District Court of Appeal, *Florida Department of Children and Families v. In re Matter of Adoption of: X.X.G. and N.R.G.*," American Psychological Association, 2009. www.apa.org. Reproduced by permission.

20% have a son or daughter under 18 years living in their home. Approximately 270,000 children were living in households headed by same-sex couples as of 2005. In Florida, Census data indicates that 17% of the households headed by a same-sex couple include children under age 18. As of 2005, approximately 17,000 Florida children were living in households headed by same-sex couples. If one includes sexual minority parents not captured in the Census data, researchers estimate that considerably more—perhaps millions of American parents and thousands of Florida parents—today identify themselves as gay, lesbian, or bisexual. In terms of adoption, a 2007 study using data from the Census and the National Survey of Family Growth (NSFG) estimated that approximately 65,500 adopted children were being raised by lesbian or gay parents. Similarly, in Florida approximately 1.2% of adopted children under 18 years (about 960 children) were living in a gay or lesbian household.

Families comprising same-sex couples and their children have diverse origins and take a variety of forms. Regardless of whether the children were adopted or were conceived in one partner's prior heterosexual relationship, through donor insemination, or with the assistance of a surrogate mother, both members of the same-sex couple typically function as parents for the children, even if they are not legally recognized as such.

Sexual Orientation Does Not Affect Suitability to Raise Children

Although it is sometimes asserted in policy debates that heterosexual couples are inherently better parents than same-sex couples, or that the children of lesbian or gay parents fare worse than children raised by heterosexual parents, those claims find no support in the scientific research literature.

When comparing the outcomes of different forms of parenting, it is critically important to make appropriate comparisons. For example, differences resulting from the *number* of parents in a household cannot be attributed to the parents' *gender* or *sexual orientation*. Research in households with heterosexual parents generally indicates that, all else being equal, children do better with two parenting figures rather than just one. However, the specific research studies typically cited in this regard do not address parents' sexual orientation and thus do not permit any conclusions about the consequences of having heterosexual versus nonheterosexual parents, or two parents who are of the same versus different genders.

Indeed, the scientific research that has directly compared outcomes for children with gay or lesbian parents with outcomes for children with heterosexual parents has been remarkably consistent in indicating that lesbian and gay parents are every bit as fit and capable as heterosexual parents, and their children are as psychologically healthy and well-adjusted as children reared by heterosexual parents. While most studies in this area have not specifically studied lesbian or gay adoptive parents, the available data do not indicate that sexual minority adoptive parents are any less fit than heterosexual adoptive parents.

[L]esbian and gay parents are every bit as fit and capable as heterosexual parents, and their children are as psychologically healthy and well-adjusted as children reared by heterosexual parents.

Empirical research over the past two decades [1990–2010] has failed to find meaningful differences in the parenting ability of lesbian and gay parents compared to heterosexual parents. Most research on this topic has focused on lesbian mothers and refutes the stereotype that lesbian parents are not as child-oriented or maternal as non-lesbian mothers. Researchers have concluded that heterosexual and lesbian mothers do not differ in their parenting ability. Relatively few published studies have directly examined gay fathers, but those that exist similarly find that gay men are as fit and able parents as heterosexual men.

Turning to the children of gay parents, a comprehensive survey of peer-reviewed scientific studies in this area reported no differences between children raised by lesbians and those raised by heterosexuals with respect to the factors that matter: self-esteem, anxiety, depression, behavioral problems, performance in social arenas (sports, school and friendships), use of psychological counseling, mothers' and teachers' reports of children's hyperactivity, unsociability, emotional difficulty, or conduct difficulty. The authors concluded that "every relevant study to date shows that parental sexual orientation per se has no measurable effect on the quality of parent-child relationships or on children's mental health or social adjustment."

Homosexual Parents Do Not Affect Children's Sexual Identity

Nor does empirical research support the misconception that having a homosexual parent affects the development of children's gender identity (i.e., the psychological sense of being male or female). Studies of the children of lesbian mothers have not found any difference from the children of heterosexual parents in their patterns of *gender identity*. As a panel of the American Academy of Pediatrics concluded after examining peer-reviewed studies, "[n]one of the more than 300 children studied to date have shown evidence of gender identity confusion, wished to be the other sex, or consistently engaged in cross-gender behavior."

Similarly, most published studies have not found reliable differences in *social gender role* conformity (i.e., adherence to cultural norms defining feminine and masculine behavior) between the children of lesbian and heterosexual mothers. Data have not been reported on the gender identity development or gender role orientation of the sons and daughters of gay fathers. . . .

Homosexuality is neither an illness nor a disability, and the mental health professions do not regard a homosexual orientation as harmful, undesirable, or requiring intervention or prevention. Currently, there is no scientific consensus about the specific factors that cause an individual to become heterosexual, homosexual, or bisexual—including possible biological, psychological, or social effects of the parents' sexual orientation. However, the available evidence indicates that the vast majority of lesbian and gay adults were raised by heterosexual parents and the vast majority of children raised by lesbian and gay parents eventually grow up to be heterosexual.

[T]he vast majority of children raised by lesbian and gay parents eventually grow up to be heterosexual.

Amicus emphasizes that the abilities of gay and lesbian persons as parents and the positive outcomes for their children are *not* areas where credible scientific researchers disagree. Thus, after careful scrutiny of decades of research in this area, APA [American Psychological Association] concluded in its *Resolution on Sexual Orientation, Parents, and Children*: "There is *no* scientific evidence that parenting effectiveness is related to parental sexual orientation: Lesbian and gay parents are as likely as heterosexual parents to provide supportive and healthy environments for their children" and that "[r]esearch has shown that adjustment, development, and psychological well-being of children is unrelated to parental sexual orientation and that the children of lesbian and gay parents are as likely as those of heterosexual parents to flourish." Thus, APA officially "opposes any discrimination based on sexual orientation in matters of adoption, child custody and visitation, foster care, and reproductive health services." It is the quality of parenting that predicts children's psychological and social adjustment, not the parents' sexual orientation or gender.

There is no scientific basis for distinguishing between same-sex couples and heterosexual couples with respect to adoption.

9

Gays and Lesbians Should Not Be Allowed to Adopt

Liberty Counsel

Liberty Counsel is a nonprofit civil liberties education and legal defense organization devoted to preserving religious liberty, the sanctity of human life, and traditional families.

Children being placed for adoption are particularly vulnerable to physical and emotional effects of stress, and so it is extremely important not only to find them permanent homes, but to find them homes that keep their best interests at heart. Research points to problematic outcomes—such as mental health issues or suicidal tendencies—for children raised by same-sex parents. Heterosexual parents, however, are associated with stable environments that promote a child's well-being. Therefore, in the best interest of children, gays and lesbians should be excluded from adoption.

Since children being placed for adoption have already suffered separation from their biological parents, it is particularly important that they be placed in an environment that is the most likely to provide stability, continuity and peace of mind.

A "conjugal family" represents that environment [according to Camille S. Williams]—"a household structure and process that is most likely to allow an adoptive child to thrive." The conjugal family has been "the preferred site for the place-

Liberty Counsel, "Amicus Curiae Brief, State of Florida Third District Court of Appeal, *Florida Department of Children and Families v. In re Matter of Adoption of: X.X.G. and N.R.G.*," Liberty Counsel, March 4, 2009. www.lc.org. Reproduced by permission.

ment of children in adoptive homes, because this family form, although imperfect in particular instances has been the most successful both historically and currently."

> Historically, and currently, the conjugal family has been, and is, the site for procreation and for childrearing; in contrast, historically and currently, same-sex couples have not been and are not, usually associated with procreation or with childrearing. In fact, same-sex couples have been and are associated with practices that impair personal and parental effectiveness, such as high-risk sexual activities, including multiple sex partners, higher rates of emotional problems and substance abuse. . . . The conjugal marital family, in contrast, has been associated with single-partner sexual activity, legal and social responsibility for children who issued from the union, and reduced risk of substance abuse, together with higher levels of physical health, emotional and familial stability and higher income levels. For these reasons, the conjugal family—not the same-sex couple—has been the norm for adoptive placements.

[P]arental sexual orientation is positively associated with the possibility that children will attain a similar orientation.

Parental Sexual Orientation Affects a Child's Development

According to the 2000 census, 99 percent, a significant numerical norm, of the coupled households in the United States consist of heterosexual couples. In addition, documented differences between children raised by same-sex parents and those raised by opposite-sex parents point to the fact that the sex of the parent or the child or both makes a difference in a child's development. For example, researchers Judith Stacey and Timothy Biblarz found:

A significantly greater proportion of young adult children raised by lesbian than heterosexual mothers in the Tasker and Golombok sample reported having had a homoerotic relationship (6 of the 25 young adults raised by lesbian mothers—24% compared with 0 of the 20 raised by heterosexual mothers). . . .

Relative to their counterparts with heterosexual parents, the adolescent and young adult girls raised by lesbian mothers appear to have been more sexually adventurous and less chaste. . . .

[P]arental sexual orientation is positively associated with the possibility that children will attain a similar orientation, and theory and common sense also support such a view. Children raised by lesbian co-parents should and do seem to grow up more open to homoerotic relationships.

Other research points to potential problematic outcomes for such children and others who might identify themselves as homosexual. For instance, one study [by David Fergusson, John Horwood, and Annette Beautrais] indicated that "[s]ame-gender sexual orientation is significantly associated with each of the suicidality measures" gauged in the study. Specifically, "gay, lesbian, and bisexual young people are at increased risk of mental health problems, with these associations being particularly evident for measures of suicidal behavior and multiple disorder[s]." Given these "significant differences in the structure and processes of married heterosexual couple households compared to unmarried opposite-sex couples, same-sex couples, polygamous and polyamorous households, to have a married couple or unmarried individual norm as a threshold for adoption is not invidious discrimination, but a rational means of legislating requirements most likely to yield the legitimate state goal of providing a stable home for adoptive children" [according to Williams].

Gender Boundaries Are Important for a Child's Well-Being

While the Circuit Court and supporters of homosexual adoption might believe that the standard family norm is "too restrictive, discriminatory," or even against the best interest of children who might otherwise be in foster care, the fact is that "keeping the conjugal family norm is a rational means to the legitimate state goal of seeking safe placement for adoptive children" [according to Williams].

Maintaining and modeling gender boundaries is important for the development of children.

Similarly, it is not discriminatory or a sign of animus for the legislature to acknowledge the inherent binary nature of human sexuality and to seek to ensure that adoptive children are placed in environments where gender boundaries will be experienced and enforced. [Mathew Staver states] "We live in a world demarcated by two genders, male and female. There is no third or intermediate category. Sex is binary." Maintaining and modeling gender boundaries is important for the development of children. Having both a mother and a father in the home provides children with four models of these boundaries: (1) A role model of a stable heterosexual marriage relationship, (2) A role model of a mother and father coordinating co-parenting, (3) A parenting role model of a father-child relationship and (4) A parenting role model of a mother-child relationship. A same-sex household de[prives children] of those four models and therefore, by [placing chil-]dren at a disadvantage. It is rational for the legislature, acting as *parens patriae*, [parent of the nation] to not place children who have already suffered loss of family relationships into an inherently disadvantageous circumstance.

It is also rational for the state to decide that it is not in the best interest of children to place them into an environment in which they are more likely to experience [according to George Rekers] "the stress and associated harm of an ill-timed sex education that is not timed to match the psychosexual developmental needs of the child," of encountering or being exposed to homosexual paraphernalia, pornography and political activity, or of being exposed to a household that does not restrict sexual relationships to marriage. . . .

[C]oncerns about sexual practices . . . that pose potential risk of harm to children cannot ethically (or legally) be ignored even if they make us uncomfortable.

Potential Risks to the Child Should Not Be Ignored

The state's *parens patriae* responsibility does not mean merely finding permanent homes for as many children as possible, but exercising diligence and discernment so that children are placed in safe environments that minimize the risk of harm. [According to Lynn Wardle] "The state and its agents have a heavy *parens patriae* duty to act in the best interests of children and to protect them from danger, when they come under their supervisory powers in adoption cases." "[V]alid concerns about sexual practices, relationships, social patterns and individual characteristics that pose potential risk of harm to children cannot ethically (or legally) be ignored even if they make us uncomfortable." Consequently, it is rational for the legislature to conclude that, in light of the vulnerability of children needing placement and the continuing disagreement among child development experts about the effects of homosexual parenting on children it is in the best interest of the children to exclude homosexuals from adoption. As William L. Pierce, the founder and longtime president of the National Council

For Adoption said:

> The best place for a child in need of placement, all things
> being equal, is a private family with parents whose health
> and lifestyles are such that they are likely to provide the
> child appropriate care and modeling at least until the child
> is 18. . . . The data suggest that a family headed by one male
> and one female who are married to each other have benefi-
> cial outcomes for children they adopt, taking into account
> proper screening, preparation, and support for the family.
> . . . Other family constellations, including un-married, long-
> term cohabiting heterosexuals, or single-parent heterosexual
> households, are less optimal for children. The data . . . do
> not tell us anything about same-sex parenting. There is a
> basic rule of prudence that should apply as a result: When
> in doubt, don't.

10

State Father Registries Can Be Unfair to Birth Fathers

Sammy Ayer

Sammy Ayer is a Juris Doctor candidate at Regent University School of Law in Virginia Beach, Virginia.

A putative father is basically an unmarried man who is presumed to be the father of a baby. Some states have created putative father registries to protect the rights of fathers. Unfortunately, the registries can actually work against biological fathers. For example, men are not always aware that they fathered a child, yet lack of knowledge of a pregnancy does not excuse a man for not filing with the registry. Also, registering in the state in which the baby was conceived does not guarantee the father will be notified of an adoption proceeding in another state.

Imagine waking up and anxiously awaiting a phone call that you know will change your life forever. You know you are about to be a proud father, so you are frantically sitting by the phone and waiting for it to ring, but the phone never makes a sound. You then decide to call your significant other to see what's going on, but her cellular phone is off. You get out of bed, brush your teeth, and rush to the hospital for the moment you have waited nearly a year for. When you finally arrive at the hospital, full of emotions, you are told by administration that no such baby and no such mother are currently there. You spend the next several days searching for your

Sammy Ayer, "Have You Seen My Daddy?: An Analytical Look at Virginia's Putative Father Statutes," Regent University School of Law, 2010. www.regent.edu. Copyright © 2010 by Sammy Ayer. All rights reserved. Reproduced by permission.

child, but can't track down her or her mother. When you finally discover the whereabouts of your first born child, it is too late, because she has been adopted by a family on the other side of the country, and you are told that your paternal rights have been terminated, and someone else now has custody of your child. Sadly, this is exactly what happened to John Wyatt in February of 2009. . . .

> *The putative father registries were designed to give unwed fathers notice of adoption proceedings pertaining to their biological child.*

How the Putative Father Registries Came About

The Virginia Putative Father Registry is a confidential database designed to protect the rights of a putative[1] father who wishes to be informed of any proceedings involving the adoption of, or termination of parental rights for a child he may have fathered. There are four ways in which you can be considered to be a putative father, 1. You are not married to the child's mother; 2. Court has not determined you are the child's father; 3. You have not signed a written agreement that acknowledges you are the child's father; and 4. You have not adopted the child. The purpose of registering is to ensure that you do not miss the opportunity to be an important part of your child's life. When you timely register, you become entitled to a proper notification of any proceedings pertaining to the termination of or adoption of the child you think you fathered. Failing to register can lead to your parental rights being terminated unbeknownst to you. . . .

Since the 1960's, the rate of children born out of wedlock has increased dramatically. Currently, in the United States 4

---

1. A putative father is an unmarried man who is presumed to be the baby's father.

out of every 10 children are born to an unwed mother. Statistics show that the children born out of wedlock are much more likely to be put up for adoption then the children born to married parents. In the late 60's and early 70's, the majority of unwed mothers were teenagers, but that trend has been significantly altered in the past few years. In the more recent years, women in their twenties and thirties have had a 34% increase in unwed births. Most analysts feel this can be attributed to the large number of unmarried couples who cohabit with one another across the country. In 2007, women in their twenties had 60% of all babies born out of wedlock, teenagers had 23%, and women over the age of thirty had the other 17%. These statistics illustrate how much of a problem unwed births are becoming for women of all ages.

When a child is born out of wedlock, there are numerous conflicting interests that have to be handled and taken into consideration when determining how to handle adoption proceedings. Basically, we have to determine the best way to protect the parental rights of the father while maintaining the privacy rights of the mother and still take into consideration what is in the best interests of the child. In the early 1990s there were three controversial court cases that were asked to analyze these exact issues when 3 unwed birth fathers contested the adoptions of their newborn children. These cases gained a lot of publicity across the country, and they played a huge role in state legislature's decision to enact putative father registries. The putative father registries were designed to give unwed fathers notice of adoption proceedings pertaining to their biological child. In order for an unwed father's parental rights to be protected, he must file a notice of intent to claim paternity through the putative father registries of the state he lives in. Sadly, registering as a putative father in the state of conception does not necessarily guarantee you will receive notice of an adoption proceeding in another state.

An Example of How the Registry Can Falter

John Wyatt and his girlfriend, Emily Fahland, had known each other since second grade and dated off and on all through high school and parts of college. When the two of them found out they were going to have a baby they each had different emotions. Fahland felt that putting the baby up for adoption was the best thing for the child, but Wyatt insisted that they could have a future and raise the baby together. Arguments over what was best for the child led the couple to become more distant then they once had been, but Fahland promised she would call Wyatt as soon as she went into labor and she said she wouldn't proceed with any type of adoptive proceedings without talking to him first. Unfortunately, when Fahland went into labor, not only did she neglect to call, but she also turned off her cell phone making it impossible for John to contact her.

> [T]he Supreme Court used the equal protection clause to rule that state laws had to treat unwed mothers and unwed fathers in a similar manner.

After repeatedly calling Fahland's phone, John finally called the hospital where the baby was to be born, and they informed him that Fahland and his daughter were both there. However, when John arrived at the hospital the story had changed and no one could find his girlfriend or his baby, Emma. That was because Fahland had already checked out of the hospital and was staying at a local hotel with an adoption agency representative from Utah. This representative along with the potential adoptive parents from Utah was helping care for both Emma and Fahland. Then, just two days after Emma was born, Fahland signed the adoption consent forms and gave custody of her and Wyatt's child to the Zarembinski's, a married couple from Utah. The Zarembinski's cared for

Emma at another local hotel for a few days before flying her out to Utah where she still resides today.

On February 18, [2009] just 8 days after Emma was born, Wyatt filed for custody of his daughter in the Stafford County Juvenile and Domestic Relations Court. Finally, in December [2009] a judge granted Wyatt custody of his young daughter whom he still had never had the chance to hold. The judge stated that because Wyatt filed for custody five days before the Zarembinski's filed their adoption papers in Utah, and because Wyatt filed within ten days of Emma's birth, he was to be awarded custody of his daughter. Unfortunately, a Utah judge ruled that the Zarembinski's could maintain custody while the adoption proceedings took place, because Wyatt failed to register on Virginia's putative father registry. The Utah judge said that Wyatt's failure to abide by Virginia putative father statutes had led to a legal and proper termination of his parental rights and his consent was not needed for the adoption to be valid. Basically, a Virginia judge held that Wyatt had complied with the states putative father statutes when he filed for custody, but the Utah judge held that filing for adoption wasn't the same as filing with the putative father registry; therefore, Wyatt had relinquished his parental rights.

The Requirements of Putative Father Registries

Up until the Supreme Court's decision in *Stanley v. Illinois*, unwed mothers were generally given the right to decide what was best for their child. In *Stanley*, the Supreme Court used the equal protection clause to rule that state laws had to treat unwed mothers and unwed fathers in a similar manner. This was a gigantic step for the biological fathers who hoped to be an influential part of their child's life. Unfortunately, ensuring the parental rights of unwed fathers, did not ensure that these men would play stable and positive roles in their children's lives, but it did help to ensure their parental rights could not be terminated without them receiving the proper notice. Creating the putative father statutes was supposed to help prevent unexpected disruptions from occurring during adoption proceedings by notifying the father that his child was going to be adopted and his parental rights terminated, if he didn't take the appropriate steps to prevent it.

Every child that is adopted is less likely to grow up in poverty, they are more likely to get a good education, they are more likely to have a participating father figure and they are more likely to grow up to be a productive member of society.

The putative father registry is established within the social services department. Putative father statutes require that a man timely file with the putative father registry in order for him to contest and receive notice of adoption proceedings pertaining to his biological child. The putative father registry is supposed to be designed to protect the parental rights of a father who has a child out of wedlock. If a father is married to, or has recently separated from, the child's mother, then he is not required to register with the putative father registry, because his parental rights are already ensured. Likewise, fathers who have established paternity through a judicial proceeding or father's who have filed to establish paternity through a judicial proceeding, are not required to file with the putative father registry, yet they are still entitled to notice of a potential adoption proceeding.

Critics of the putative father registry argue that it is difficult for men to know when a child is conceived during intercourse with someone whom no long term commitment has been made. Under Virginia law, a man is considered to have legal notice that he could be a father as soon as he has sexual intercourse with a woman. Since sex is the equivalent of notice, men are required to file in the Virginia putative father registry within ten days of the child's birth, or else their parental rights could be terminated and they would be left with no legal right to object to an adoption proceeding involving their biological child. Lack of knowledge of the pregnancy does not excuse a man from timely filing with the putative father registry. However, this ten day registration deadline does not apply to putative father's whose identities are "reasonably ascertainable." When the putative father's identity is "reasonably ascertainable," notice of the mother's adoption plan must be served on him and he then has ten days, from the date the notice was mailed to him, to file on the putative father registry and challenge the adoption proceeding. . . .

With the economy crumbling, adoption has become an incredibly important issue in the United States. Every child that is adopted is less likely to grow up in poverty, they are more likely to get a good education, they are more likely to have a participating father figure and they are more likely to grow up to be a productive member of society. Obviously, this isn't always the case, but it is shown to be true in a vast majority of the cases analyzed. Statistics also show that children who grow up without a father figure are two to three more times likely to do poorly in school, they are two to three times more likely to have emotional or behavioral problems at school, they are more likely to commit crimes as juveniles, and they are more likely to engage in premarital sexual activity. These statistics help to show how adoptions can make a significant impact on the children as well as the economy. However, it is still essential that biological parents have a say in whether or not they want to raise their children themselves or put them up for adoption. The major criticism of the putative father registries used today is that they fail to take the necessary steps to inform a registrant that his parental rights could be terminated and his child given to another family to be raised.

11

A National Father Registry Would Protect the Rights of Birth Fathers

Mary M. Beck

Mary M. Beck is the director of the Domestic Violence Clinic and Clinical Professor of Law at the University of Missouri School of Law.

The Supreme Court has held that an unwed father has a right to be notified of any adoption petition regarding his biological child. To protect that right, some states have created putative father registries, which mandate that men register if they believe they have fathered a child. In return, the registry would notify the father of adoption proceedings. These state registries, however, resolve paternity issues only within a particular state; should the mother relocate to another state or the adoption petition originate in a state in which the father has not registered, the father might not be notified. A National Putative Father Registry would solve the problem of interstate travel, protect the father's right to notification, and advance the best interests of the child by expediting the adoption process.

Over one-third of all births are to unwed parents. Adoption proceedings for these children can be delayed, contested, and disrupted when paternity is in question. Highly

Mary M. Beck, "A National Putative Father Registry," Center for Family Policy & Research, 2007. mucenter.missouri.edu. Copyright © 2007 by Mary Beck. All rights reserved. Reproduced by permission.

publicized court cases, such as Baby Jessica's [in 1993] in which an unwed birth father contested her adoption and then initiated litigation, alerted the general public to this issue. Although state Putative Father Registries resolve paternity issues for in-state adoptions, only federal legislation creating a national registry can expedite permanency for children in interstate adoptions.

[F]athers register if they believe they have fathered a child.

What Is a Putative Father Registry?

Some 33 state legislatures have enacted Paternity Registries but only 23 avert disrupted adoptions by the late assertion of paternal rights. A Putative Father Registry mandates that unwed fathers mail in a postcard to register their possible claim for paternity rights in a timely manner. Registration insures fathers' notification of an adoption petition. These registries assist fathers in asserting paternity and assuming related parental duties *or* foreclose their paternal rights. In operation, fathers register if they believe they have fathered a child. Should the mother make an adoption plan, the registry provides notification to the father of the possible adoption. Thus, the father can participate in the adoption, default on the petition, or pursue his paternal rights at or before the initial adoption hearing. Adoption proceedings can then commence without the possibility of disruption due to late paternity claims. The privacy and safety of the mother is secured because she does not have to identify the possible father nor inform the father of her pregnancy. The privacy of the father is protected in that notice is mailed only to the secure address he has provided the registry. Both mother's and father's privacy are protected in that no names are published in the newspaper.

What Are the Stipulations Regarding Father Registries?

The Supreme Court has held on three occasions that unwed fathers are constitutionally entitled to notice of adoption proceedings of children with whom they have established relationships. State law entitles unwed fathers to notice if they meet statutory criteria. Thus, unwed fathers' established relationships and/or endeavors to assume parental responsibility provide grounds for notice and opportunities to be heard regarding pending adoptions. Putative Father Registries affect paternal rights to newborns as well as older children. Questions arise as to what constitutes a relationship with a newborn and evidence of assuming paternal responsibilities. To address these issues, and related legal issues, court decisions and state laws provide that:

- Registries are constitutional and do not deny father's due process or equal protection.

- A timely registered unwed father is insured notice at the address he provided the registry.

- Fathers bear the burden of registering in a timely manner. Failure to do so can be viewed as pre-birth abandonment and, therefore, grounds to foreclose the father's rights.

- The period of pregnancy plus a defined number of days after birth is adequate time for unwed fathers to protect paternity rights and to indicate their interest and ability to assume parental responsibilities.

- Notice of pending adoptions is not required for unwed fathers who have not filed or not filed in a timely manner with the Putative Father Registry or otherwise established paternity legally.

- Sexual intercourse serves as notice of possible conception. A lack of knowledge of a pregnancy or birth does not constitute an acceptable reason for failing to register.

These decisions hold that unwed fathers have an inchoate interest in their child that they can transform into a constitutionally protected interest if they assume parental responsibilities. The decisions also indicate that states have an overarching goal to advance the best interest of children, provide children with stable homes, and avoid the disruption of adoption proceedings.

A National Putative Father Registry would address the problems associated with interstate travel.

State Putative Father Registries can alleviate problems in which the adoption petition is filed in the state of conception. However, due to interstate travel, births and adoption proceedings can occur in a state unknown to the unwed father. In such cases, paternity rights can be thwarted even if the father has filed with the Putative Father Registry in the state of conception. When interstate travel occurs and paternity rights are asserted late through litigation, a child's adoptive placement can be disrupted or an earnest father's rights extinguished.

How Would a National Putative Father Registry Work?

A National Putative Father Registry would address the problems associated with interstate travel. The registry would have the dual purpose of expediting secure adoptive placements and facilitating notice of adoption proceedings to unwed birth fathers in interstate adoptive situations. The registry would also advance the privacy of mothers and fathers; address the safety interests of mothers; facilitate planning for children;

clarify the rights of birth fathers; encourage fathers to assume personal parental responsibility; reduce time in foster care; and, save states' money.

The development of a National Putative Father Registry is facilitated by uniform state registries. Such registries would include the following elements:

1. Define categories of fathers as presumed, adjudicated, acknowledged, and putative. (A putative father is defined as a man who has had sexual relations with a woman and is therefore on notice that she may become pregnant as a result of those relations.)

2. Establish a time limit for unwed fathers' registration and insure notice of adoption &/or child abuse and neglect actions to timely registered unwed fathers (as well as presumed, adjudicated, or acknowledged fathers).

3. Protect the privacy and safety of mothers by relieving mothers of the responsibility to notify the father of pregnancy or to notify the courts of the identities of possible fathers.

4. Protect the privacy of birth mothers and fathers by not publishing their names in the newspaper.

5. Require unwed fathers to legally establish paternity and assume parental responsibilities during pregnancy and the period immediately following birth in order to protect their paternal rights.

6. Set consequences for the putative father who does not file timely and establish legal paternity.

7. Amend long arm statutes to assert personal jurisdiction over the registered putative fathers.

8. Establish saving provisions to protect the earnest father who is defrauded by a mother.

9. Regulate who can access and search the Putative Father Registry to ensure the privacy of all parties.

12

Birth Certificates of Adoptees Should Not Be Amended

Amanda Woolston

Amanda Woolston, an adoptee and former social services coordinator, created the blog Declassified Adoptee *in dedication to adoption reform and family preservation. Woolston's articles have appeared in many publications and news services.*

The practice of amending birth certificates of adopted children was originally intended to protect adoptive families from any potential interference from biological families, and to protect adopted children from the "stigma" of their origins. But amending vital statistical information and passing it off as fact actually causes more harm than good; it is an unethical policy and is disrespectful to the adopted child, the biological parents, the adoptive parents, and to society at large. Furthermore, preventing adoptees access to accurate birth records sets them apart and can cause them to feel inferior to people who are not adopted.

"Why would they lie?" I thought to myself when I first saw my amended birth certificate. I was 11 or 12 and it was out on the kitchen counter for some reason I don't recall. I was alone in the room at the time, wondering if I was allowed to look at the document. I didn't know my first mother's name, no one had ever told me before. So I wondered, am I allowed to know? Feeling very brave and rebellious, I took a peek only to be taken aback that it did not con-

Amanda Woolston, "Why My [Amended] Birth Certificate Is a Lie," *Declassified Adoptee* (blog), June 6, 2011. www.declassifiedadoptee.com. Copyright © 2011 by Declassified Adoptee. All rights reserved. Reproduced by permission.

tain my first mother's name at all. There it was, "certificate of live birth" from the state of Tennessee with my birth date, my name, my place of birth . . . yet my adoptive parents were listed in place of my first mother's name. I couldn't believe it. I vaguely remember asking my mom why she and my father were on my birth certificate and received a "we're your parents" sort of response and feeling like my question had not quite been answered.

A Conflict About Truth

Many thoughts went through my mind. "Did the State save her name before they took it off?" "Has my choice to one day know her name been taken away from me? Why couldn't someone have asked what I wanted?" "Why would you put wrong information about my birth on my birth certificate?" "Is there something wrong with where I come from that it has to be hidden like that?" Of course, I had no concept of what an original was, that it was sealed, and that this wasn't really my factual birth document. I didn't learn about that until my early 20's. My sense of injustice from seeing this "birth certificate" was not about me weighing in on who my "real parents" are. Rather, I felt a conflict between the lesson of the truth being important when there were exceptions to the rule. But what, however, was it about adoption that there was an exception to telling and knowing the truth?

When a child is born, the State government collects and keeps vital statistics information. It makes various pieces of this information available to the person who was born in the form of a birth certificate. Birth certificates are government recorded and issued documents that contain the vital statistics information collected at the time of the persons' birth.

In my journey in Adoptee Rights activism, I have encountered several points people will make in defense to the amending and even sealing of a birth certificate. Some say that it is easier to have one amended certificate with the adoptive parents names on it. Some say that amending and sealing is necessary so that no one will have to know that someone is adopted unless the family or the adopted person decide to disclose it to others.

Some say that the amended certificate isn't untruthful at all. Despite the fact that it says "certificate of live birth" and contains birth information, "mother" and "father" having the adoptive parents names is correct because they are mother and father. I suppose because it doesn't specifically state "mother who gave birth" or "father who fathered the child." And some will flat out state that the birth certificate should not have the original parents on it and ought to have the adoptive parents instead because they're the real parents, the ones who did all the hard work, and they deserve to be acknowledged on a birth certificate.

They might also point out that birth and biology are no longer synonymous because of surrogacy and donor conception and that, therefore, adoptees cannot claim a right to know biology and birth information through their birth certificates because of that.

When there is a different rule for adoption, we assert that there is something inherently wrong with being adopted.

A "Birth" Certificate Should Have "Birth" Information

It certainly is not easier for many adopted persons in adulthood to have an amended certificate and not their original—just ask those who cannot get passports and driver's licenses, to name just a few complications. Also, want to compare your amended to the original to verify that you know correct information about yourself? Want to know your first parents' names? Tough cookies. Adoptees in 44 States have a great deal of difficulty doing so.

Birth certificates are not "hide your family drama" certificates. They are *birth* certificates. During his childhood, my father had no amended birth certificate to hide that his mother did not raise him or his brother since the ages of one and two. My grandfather could not have amended his birth certificate to hide that his mother sent him to live at a boarding school for "fatherless boys" after his dad died while keeping his brother. Foster kids do not have their birth certificates amended and sealed to hide that they are not being raised by their first parents. No one else, regardless of the situation, has their birth certificate amended and sealed. Adoption should be no exception. When there is a different rule for adoption, we assert that there is something inherently wrong with being adopted.

Adoptees deserve the same birth documentation all others get.

As for what "mother" and "father" are intended to mean on the birth certificate, I think that the fact that the document is kept and recorded by the Vital Statistics office, and contains all information pertaining to birth, "mother" and "father" generally speaking on anything claiming to be a "birth certificate" are clearly intending to indicate the mother who gave birth and the biological father. Specifications of "mother who gave birth" and "biological father" on the birth certificate to make it clear as to whom is being referred to are superfluous. My amended birth certificate is not a redacted version of a certificate containing both birth/biological *and* adoptive information that I have full, unrestricted access to. It does not indicate that it is not the original or that information on it has been changed to include information other than birth information so that I can be aware and informed that I do not have the same birth certificate others do. There is nothing on it that indicates to me that I am adopted. When I request a birth certificate from Vital Statistics, they don't address me as an adopted person and ask me "which one?"—No, they send me this one. *Only* this one. They do not inform me another is on file. If I haven't been told I am adopted, I will not know about it. I will not know by looking at my birth certificate that it is not all birth information like *most others* have. It is a replacement birth certificate where the original is sealed from view, where I have to know about the original, know how to apply to see the original, have to pay hundreds of dollars to apply to see the original, and have to have an official letter of permission from the state government to see the original. It in every way shape and form presents my adoptive parents as being the parents who gave birth to me; period.

Again, not being on my birth certificate does not mean my parents are not my parents. It has *nothing* to do with that.

Again, we're talking about *birth certificates* here, not "I'm the real parent" certificates. Adoptees deserve the same birth documentation all others get. Period. And it shouldn't be made to be about anyone or anything else, or any other issue. *My* birth, *my* record, *my* right. The notion that birth documents are to be altered to show which family the adoptee belongs to more or which family is more entitled to claim the adoptee is perhaps the most absurd and offensive of all. This type of talk is appropriate for discussing property and possessions, not people. . . .

My "birth certificate" isn't even all that bad as compared to those of other adoptees (and some have no birth certificate of any kind at all). The "birth certificates" of many other adoptees out there have been found to contain incorrect information such as anything from the wrong race (race changed to the adoptive parents race), to the wrong birth place (claiming the adoptee was born where the adoptive parents live), to even the wrong birth date. I am fortunate to have had little discrepancy from one document to the other.

Besides the fact that it presents my adoptive parents as the parents who gave birth, there is other information on my amended birth certificate that is not correct.

In plan print, it claims to be the true and original document on file with the Vital Statistics office. As someone who has been granted the legal privilege of accessing not only my uncensored adoption file as well as access to my original birth certificate (and my hospital long-form), I can tell you that my amended birth certificate is not the true and original document on file. . . .

The origins of amending and sealing are steeped in shame and stigma . . .

Amending Birth Certificates Is Disrespectful

My first mother, who did not know about amending and sealing, was also shocked I didn't know her name. It was hard for me to have to tell her "no, I didn't, because my parents names took the place of yours and the one with your name on it was sealed." It was when I had to explain this whole process to my first mother, a real person with real feelings who is proud of all of her descendants, that I realized just how disrespectful amending and sealing is—and not just to me as the adopted person.

And no, I don't think amending and sealing is respectful of my parents either, if you're wondering.

The problem is, my birth certificate is a lie because it was never intended to be the truth. It was intended to take the place of my original birth certificate and to present itself as any other birth certificate in every way, "as if born to" my adoptive parents. It flat out substitutes biological fact with legal fiction and expects me to be none-the-wiser.

Why?? (and the answer to that is also the answer to why they are amended and sealed to begin with.) Georgia Tann was the first adoption worker to convince the Tennessee Vital Statistics Office to amend and seal the birth certificates for her adoptions. As some of you know, Tann's adoptions were illegal, all 5,000 of them. She pushed for the anonymity of the adoptee and of the adoptive parents by issuing the adopted person a new birth certificate, claiming it would protect the adoptive family from interference from the original family as well as protect the adopted person from the stigma of their impoverished and illegitimate origins by making it appear as though the child had been born to married parents. In actuality, she was trying to leave as little recourse as possible for original families to find and reclaim their children who had been unlawfully removed by Tann. Tann's goal was to handle adoptions across the United States and her push for policies of secrecy spread far and wide. Alabama was first to make amending and sealing an official act of the state for all its adoptions (it is now an open access state). Tann's stomping ground, Tennessee, was second (Tennessee is now an open access state for adoptees of Tann's era and conditional open access state for those born after Tann's era). The practice of sealing Original Birth Certificates [OBCs] spread to all the States but two, Alaska and Kansas.

And these laws are still on the books folks. The sealed OBC law in New York, for example, is nearing its 80's birthday. This law was no doubt influenced by Tann herself, as the governor who signed it into law adopted two children from her.

The origins of amending and sealing are steeped in shame and stigma and horrendously unethical practices. In my opinion, the modern day justifications not only fall short but do not erase how sincerely offensive it is to me to have amended and sealed birth certificates that were not designed for my ease and comfort but to hide who I am and where I come from, because it isn't good enough by society's standards. . . .

Truthfulness Is the Better Policy

And of course, it is just plain invalidating and insulting to be a grown adult and be lied to. Period. Not only does the amended birth certificate present a lie but it allows adoptees to continue to be lied to about being adopted altogether. And yes, this still happens in this day and age. Just a few days ago. I had a friend, who recently found out I am adopted, inquire if I was a Late Discovery Adoptee (abbreviated "LDA," and no, I'm not one) and ask me numerous questions about LDAs and about being adopted in general. Why? Because she has a friend who hasn't told her daughter she is adopted yet.

We really can do better. There is a way to provide adoptees, donor conceived persons, and those born to surrogate mothers with as much information as the average biologically-raised/non-adopted person gets when requesting a birth certificate. There is no need for amending and sealing of birth documents for the adopted. I think Australia gets the closest to having this right. Court records, birth certificates, and adoption files are all made available to adult adoptees. Birth certificates contain both birth and adoptive information. A person who does not want to share the entire contents of their birth certificate can *choose* to request a redacted copy. As for donor conception. New Zealand is an example of one country the United States could learn from in terms of birth certificates as biological, birth, and parentage information is all contained on the birth certificate. The United Kingdom, which has outlawed anonymous egg/sperm donation, is considering similar reforms (and already also allows adopted persons to receive their original birth certificates upon reaching the age of majority). We can do better too; we really can. We can do better than handing certificates to people with information that is not correct and expecting them not to feel slighted. We *can* do better than that.

13

Adoption Programs Should Promote the Needs of Older Youth

Alicia Groh

Alicia Groh, an independent consultant, specializes in child advocacy and has written various materials on child welfare policy and strategies.

Every youth in foster care needs a permanent family, yet the number of youth who age out (meaning reach the age of eighteen without being adopted) is rising steadily. This is due in part because of barriers within the child welfare system itself. For example, youth who plan to go to college or want to develop skills for living on their own are often deprived of adoption services. Also, rules that exclude facility staff members and single or older adults from the adoption process further decrease an older youth's chance of being adopted.

According to the most recent federal data, 129,000 of the 510,000 children in foster care in the United States are waiting to be adopted. This number, already too high, does not even account for those children for whom no one is looking for a family. These are youth whose parental rights have been terminated who are older than age 16 and who have a case goal of emancipation; they are excluded from the official count of waiting children.

Alicia Groh, "It's Time to Make Older Youth Adoption a Reality: Because Every Child and Youth Deserves a Family," North American Council on Adoptable Children (NACAC), November 2009. www.nacac.org. Copyright © 2009 by North American Council on Adoptable Children. All rights reserved. Reproduced by permission.

Younger foster children have a much better chance of finding a permanent family. Once waiting children in foster care are nine or older, they are much less likely to be adopted. About 43 percent of waiting children are nine or older, but 72 percent of those who are adopted are under age nine. The average age of children when they are adopted from foster care is 6.6 years, while the average age of waiting children is 8.2 years. The average waiting child has been in foster care for more than three years (39.4 months). Every day that a waiting child remains in foster care, his chances of being adopted decrease.

Once youth age out of foster care, they face extraordinary obstacles to achieving stability and well-being.

Aging Out of Foster Care

While most children leave foster care to a permanent family, either through reunification with birth parents, placement with other relatives, or adoption, an alarming number of youth exit care without any family at all. In fiscal year (FY) 2006, 26,517 youth (9 percent of all youth exiting care) aged out of care without a permanent family (also known as emancipation). The number of youth aging out each year has grown dramatically, increasing by 53 percent since 1998 (when 17,310 youth aged out).

Studies repeatedly reveal grim outcomes for youth who age out of foster care. These youth are more likely to be involved with the criminal justice system, to become teenage parents, experience homelessness, and use drugs and alcohol. They are less likely to graduate from high school and much less likely to complete college. Once youth age out of foster care, they face extraordinary obstacles to achieving stability and well-being. As these youth live on their own, without the support from family that most youth have well beyond age 18, they are less likely than their peers to be employed, more likely to have poor health outcomes, and are at greater risk for experiencing violence. . . .

For many youth who age out, the path away from a permanent family is forged years before they turn 18, due to a combination of barriers—biases against the idea that older youth can be adopted, financial disincentives to adopting older youth, policies that allow use of a permanency goal that provides no legal permanence, and policies and practices that allow teens to opt out of permanency planning efforts even when a permanent family is in their best interests. . . .

Despite being responsible for achieving permanent families for youth in its care, the child welfare system's structure imposes multiple barriers to connecting older waiting youth with adoptive families, frequently as an unplanned consequence of well-intentioned policies and laws. These system barriers can have far-reaching effects as they reinforce the misconception among child welfare professionals that it is okay to give up on finding families for older youth.

[Y]outh who receive life skills preparation support may receive no services to find them a family.

Permanency Goals That Deny Permanence

Each child in foster care is required to have a permanency plan as part of their case plan, specifying whether the goal is reunification, adoption, legal guardianship or other placement with a relative, or, if the other options have been ruled out, another planned permanent living arrangement (APPLA).

The use of independent living and APPLA as permanency goals for youth denies them a forever family. In reality, APPLA is commonly used as simply another term for long-term foster care or emancipation. In most cases, a plan of APPLA fails to provide permanence, since the placement—whether in a foster family, group home, or other form of congregate care—ceases to be the youth's home as soon as he ages out of foster care.

Similarly, allowing workers to stop efforts to find a permanent family for a youth and simply transition the youth to an independent living path sustains the misconception within the child welfare field that there are some children who simply cannot be matched with an adoptive family.

A goal of independent living, APPLA, or emancipation is essentially a plan to leave the youth disconnected and extraordinarily vulnerable. According to federal data, more than 74,000 youth in foster care have case plan goals of emancipation or long-term foster care. Without dramatic changes, these youth will almost certainly age out of foster care without a secure connection to a permanent family. . . .

Unfortunately, most child welfare agencies have separate tracks for youth with the goal of independent living and youth with permanency plans for adoption or guardianship. As a result, youth who receive life skills preparation support may receive no services to find them a family. Youth with plans for adoption or guardianship are likely to lose out on useful life skills preparation and services.

One of the largest unintended consequences of the expansion of independent living services has been the creation of additional disincentives to older youth adoption. Many youth, particularly those who are already ambivalent about adoption, fear that being adopted means they will lose out on important educational, social, and financial opportunities. For example, a variety of federal and state programs provide college tuition waivers and scholarships to former foster youth. Although some programs are available to youth adopted from care, others are limited to youth who are still in foster care when they turn 18 or graduate from high school. Youth who want to go to college face an especially complicated and potentially heartbreaking analysis, weighing the benefits of having a permanent family against expanded access to financial aid and tuition vouchers that would make college affordable.

The federal Fostering Connections to Success and Increasing Adoptions Act of 2008 ensured that youth who are adopted after 16 are eligible for independent living services, but teens adopted before their 16th birthday can still lose out on these valuable services. For other benefits, such as some states' college tuition waivers, youth must have still been in foster care as of their 14th birthday to be eligible. Under another new federal law, youth have a financial incentive to not be adopted before they turn 13. With so much variation in eligibility requirements across programs and varying ages at which being adopted might jeopardize a youth's benefits from various programs, youth in foster care, their workers, and prospective adoptive parents face a confusing set variables to weigh when considering adoption. . . .

Restrictions Blocking Prospective Parents from Adopting

The National Association of Social Workers' code of ethics provides important guidelines about how social workers can avoid conflicts of interest and prevent dual or multiple relationships with clients. This conflict of interest provision is frequently relied on by child welfare organizations to restrict workers and other staff from adopting youth in their care. Although these guidelines exist to protect both the social worker and children, they can also prevent adults who know a youth best from being able to consider adopting the youth.

For youth in congregate care facilities, these restrictions can be particularly damaging, since facility staff may be the primary adults in the youth's lives. The vast majority of youth adopted from foster care are adopted by their foster parents or relatives, but youth who are placed in congregate care facilities do not have foster parents who might adopt them. The adults that they do build relationships with are house parents, counselors, cooks, and other staff. These adults may be great resources for permanency for youth, but official and unofficial policies discourage them from adopting the youth.

One of the keys to being able to achieve permanent families for older foster youth is developing a sufficient pool of appropriate prospective adoptive parents. Laws and policies that prohibit entire categories of adults—such as those excluding prospective parents based on age, marital status, sexual orientation, or family size—from adopting create an unnecessary barrier to achieving youth permanence.

Research and experience have demonstrated that diverse kinds of families can be successful parents to foster youth; ruling out categories of adults from adopting harms youth who are waiting for a permanent family. Studies have found that gay and lesbian prospective parents in particular are very willing to adopt youth with special needs—including older youth—potentially more so than heterosexual prospective adoptive parents, so laws prohibiting them from becoming adoptive parents are excluding a pool of potential parents for the very youth who are most in need of a permanent family.

Far too frequently, the child welfare system operates in a way that makes it harder for older youth to achieve permanence. Sometimes professionals—social workers, judges, attorneys, administrators, and others—give up on trying to achieve a permanent family for older youth. In some cases, this attitude is based on a desire to shield youth from the emotional trauma of another move or rejection. In other cases, social workers and other professionals believe that youth are doing well enough in their current placement and don't want to disrupt the youth's life. Older youth may also lose out on being adopted because some child welfare professionals neglect to understand and address both youth's and prospective adoptive parents' concerns and misconceptions about older youth adoption.

Misconceptions About Adopting Older Youth

The misconception that older youth are unadoptable still remains, despite years of organizations' successfully placing teens in permanent adoptive families. A 1999 study of foster youth in New York state who had been waiting the longest to be adopted revealed a widespread, discouraging attitude among workers and agencies that the youth were unadoptable: "Approximately 67 percent of caseworkers and 69 percent of agencies in this study were not convinced about the adoptability of the child in their care." When social workers—the very people whose job it is to find families for waiting children—and other child welfare professionals give up on the idea of achieving a permanent family for older youth, how can we expect youth to hold onto hope of finding a forever family?

Time and time again, we hear from youth that they are concerned that being adopted will mean that they won't be able to hold onto their relationships with people who are important to them, especially their birth parents and siblings. The fear of losing those connections can discourage youth from wanting to be adopted. When workers discount or fail to address youth's fears about losing connections with relatives, they risk keeping in place a major barrier to achieving permanence for youth.

Margaret Burke, director of the Family Connections Project in Illinois, which received a federal grant to help youth retain contact with family members during permanency efforts, explained:

> Many youth aren't interested in adoption if they can't maintain their relationships with their birth families. They don't want to be put in a position of having to choose one family over the other. Older youth especially may have strong attachments to parents, siblings, extended family, and even to foster siblings or former foster parents. Agencies need to safeguard these attachments and ensure that adoptive fami-

lies can help their teens maintain these ties through an open adoption. If youth know that they aren't going to lose their relationships with their birth families and other important people, they are more willing to consider adoption or guardianship.

---

45 percent of Americans incorrectly believe that children in foster care are there because they are juvenile delinquents.

Child welfare professionals have to help prospective adoptive parents decide if they can parent an older youth. Many prospective adoptive parents begin the adoption process interested in adopting a younger child. A recent study reaffirmed the widespread preference among prospective adopters for younger children, with most wanting to adopt a child under age 11. This preference can reinforce older youth's beliefs that adults don't want to adopt them:

> The general consensus among the youth ... was that no one wants to adopt teenagers. ... Some youth suggested that people think teenagers in the foster care system are 'bad' or that there must be 'something wrong with them' if they have been in multiple placements. Another youth suggested that the media portrayed youth in a negative light, such as 'doing drugs and stealing cars,' which may deter prospective families from wanting to adopt teenagers. The youth felt that people would rather adopt younger children for multiple reasons, including this perception that all teenagers in the foster care system are 'bad.'

These perceptions by older youth echo a far-too-common misconception among the public about the youth in foster care—a 2007 national survey revealed that 45 percent of Americans incorrectly believe that children in foster care are there because they are juvenile delinquents. With such negative views of foster youth and widespread negative attitudes in society about teenagers in general, workers face challenges in recruiting and retaining prospective adoptive parents who will be open to adopting older youth and helping prospective parents address both their misconceptions and very valid concerns about the needs of waiting youth in foster care. . . .

Understanding the policy and practice barriers that prevent older youth from being adopted is only the first step; we must break down these barriers and ensure that the child welfare system's laws, policies, and practices facilitate true permanency for every child and youth that it serves. . . .

14

Post-Adoption Services Need to Be Improved

Susan Livingston Smith

Susan Livingston Smith is the program and project director of the Evan B. Donaldson Adoption Institute, a nonprofit organization dedicated to improving and strengthening adoption law, policies, and practices.

The vast majority of adoptive families are highly satisfied with their adoptions. But in America today, many adopted children come from foster care or international institutions; as a result, these children are at risk for developmental, health, emotional, and behavioral issues. To help adopted children adjust to their new environment and to support them as they grow and mature, post-adoption counseling and therapeutic services should be available to them throughout their life cycles. Some adoptive parents are also in need of educational and supportive services to address specific difficulties and to strengthen their coping abilities. With the goal of successful, long-lasting adoptions and the well-being of adopted children, federal, state, and local governments need to work together to provide these vital post-adoption services.

Adoption clearly benefits children who otherwise would grow up in less stable and nurturing situations; however, many boys and girls have higher risks for ongoing develop-

Susan Livingston Smith, "Keeping the Promise: The Critical Need for Post-Adoption Services to Enable Children and Families to Succeed," Evan B. Donaldson Adoption Institute, October 2010. www.adoptioninstitute.org. Copyright © 2010 by Evan B. Donaldson Adoption Institute. All rights reserved. Reproduced by permission.

mental issues before their adoptions. Even children adopted in early infancy, who were at one time thought to come to their families as "clean slates," are seen more frequently in clinical populations than are peers raised in their families of origin. In this report we include an overview of research on variables linked with both positive and problematic adoption outcomes, because understanding these dynamics is essential for assessing families' needs after adoption and for gaining insights into the complexities of solutions for meeting those needs. . . .

The range of services needed to sustain adoptive families includes preventive, supportive, and therapeutic services.

Adoption Is a Lifelong Process

This basic tenet of adoption—that it is an ongoing, evolving experience and not a one-time occurrence—has major implications for the field of post-adoption services. A range of services should be available throughout the life cycles of adopted individuals and their families to educate and support parents to meet the needs of their children and to provide adoption-sensitive therapeutic interventions if difficulties arise. The field of specialized post-adoption services is relatively young; practitioners have struggled to know what services best meet families' needs and to make these services available to the many families who want them. The recommendations below address critical needs for the continued development of post-adoption services and for the reshaping of law, policy and practice to enable children and families who need assistance to receive it in a timely manner in order to maximize successful adoptions.

The range of services needed to sustain adoptive families includes preventive, supportive, and therapeutic services. Preventive services such as education and information assist families in understanding their child and family situation and in learning the most effective strategies for parenting. Supportive services such as information and referral, support groups, respite care, and advocacy help to normalize their view of their situation, relieve ongoing stress, strengthen their coping abilities, and assist them in obtaining needed resources for their family. Finally, a minority of adoptive families need clinical interventions to address specific difficulties, including specialized assessment services, crisis intervention, a variety of therapeutic interventions, and, for some, residential treatment services that include the adoptive family in treatment efforts.

Not all adoptive families will need or desire post-adoption services, and some will avail themselves of educational opportunities through books, adoption magazines, or the internet; however, many of them will struggle and would benefit from adoption-competent services. Development of knowledge on post-adoption practice and development of services for these families is the primary challenge to assure permanency for children removed from their birth families and to help them develop to their fullest potential. In order to promote progress in these areas, we make the following recommendations.

A national task force needs to provide strategic planning and legislative leadership for the development of post-adoption services; the body should include representatives from the Children's Bureau of the U.S. Department of Health and Human Services and the Department of State, as well as post-adoption experts, practitioners, and researchers. The task force should collect information, discuss key issues, and draft proposals/legislation to promote additional funding, policy changes, and practice improvements. This needs to be a long-term, sustained initiative to ensure that the effort is not ephemeral, but brings about continuing progress.

Support Children and Educate Parents

Many children placed from foster care or institutions here or abroad have negative past experiences that pose risks to ongoing healthy development. To truly promote successful adoptions, we need to minimize the damage that children experience on their paths to adoption, both in the U.S. and in orphanages abroad. Providing responsive and sensitive nurturance to children after separation from birth families, minimizing their moves in care or their number of caretakers, finding the right homes early in their journeys, and supporting them through transitions in care are all aspects of this goal. Some international efforts have already begun to move children from orphanages into foster homes and to provide better care for those remaining in institutions. Within the U.S. foster care system, it is important to use best practices to identify responsible relatives before children are removed, to utilize concurrent planning to place them into families that could become permanent resources if they are unable to return to their original homes, and to maximize placements with all their siblings in order to reduce traumatic losses. Assisting children to address loss and trauma issues includes supporting them through moves that must occur, maintaining their connections to significant attachment figures to the extent possible, and providing therapeutic opportunities for them to make sense of and cope with the events in their lives. . . .

It also is important to stress their need for contact with other adoptive families.

Families seeking to adopt, as well as those who already have adopted, need meaningful educational opportunities to understand the risk and protective factors in adoptive families, as well as the issues that may emerge over their child's development. . . . Individual preparation of families includes helping them to understand the specific child whom they are adopting and to forecast potential needs of the child in light of his/her history and known issues. These efforts help parents to have realistic expectations of their child and themselves. It also is important to assist adoptive families in identifying both informal and formal support systems to address their needs and link them with supports that are not readily available.

Another vital aspect of preparation is educating parents about the range and benefits of post-adoption services and normalizing help-seeking, reframing this as a parental strength and not a weakness. It also is important to stress their need for contact with other adoptive families, not only for their own support, but also for their children to have these supportive relationships. This is a particularly valuable resource for children adopted transracially who may have few connections to others from their same race/ethnicity. . . .

Educate Professionals to Understand Adoption

Teachers, school counselors, school psychologists, medical professionals, social workers and other mental health professionals need to be provided with adoption-related training that will sensitize them to critical issues adopted children and adoptive parents confront in interacting with these systems. They are the frontline of helpers to whom parents go for advice and guidance in addressing the needs of their children, and they need greater awareness of the range of risk factors that impact the adjustment of some adopted children as well as normative challenges these youth face. . . .

Although professionals cannot always predict the children who are high risk for later adjustment difficulties, there are definitely indicators evidenced through research. Some of these include children with high levels of oppositional, defiant behaviors, difficulty giving and receiving affection, histories of severe maltreatment, many moves in care, diagnosed effects of substance exposure, or significant mental illness in their family histories. Providing preventive and early intervention services to families adopting these children is extremely important in stabilizing these adoptions. The means for accomplishing this goal is more readily available for state agencies placing children from foster care; however, families adopting internationally also need to be able to access such services for high-risk children, perhaps on a fee basis.

Preventive and early intervention services to families adopting these children are extremely important in helping these adoptions be successful. Providing a time-limited intervention, such as the 18-week program, ARC (Attachment, Self-Regulation, & Competency), would help new adoptive families gain a firm foundation to address their children's needs. Hopefully, provision of such services would mean that problems do not intensify and patterns do not become entrenched for a period of years before families seek help. . . .

Families with serious needs require therapeutic interventions from highly skilled professionals . . .

Keep the Promise

States need to take a leadership role in assessing the current continuum of post-adoption services and work with stakeholders to create a strategic plan for development of a comprehensive continuum of services. In strengthening adoption-competent counseling services, a range of strategies are needed. While specialized post-adoption services have grown in many states, it is unlikely that these programs will ever be sufficient to meet the counseling needs of all adoptive families. Many programs only serve child welfare adoptive families, and in no state are these programs comprehensive enough or accessible enough to meet the ongoing counseling needs of all adoptive families. We need to find innovative ways to provide training to the range of mental health professionals, both within their educational programs and afterwards. These professionals work in an array of community settings, including family counseling agencies, private practices, mental health clinics, child welfare agencies, and others. There are now about

10 adoption certification programs that train 20–30 professionals, on average, a year. These programs, even if doubled,
cannot reach the hundreds of thousands of mental health
professionals who work with adoptive families. Additional
strategies are needed, such as web-based training linked with
CEUs [continuing education units] or other innovations.

A strategic plan involving collaboration among state human services systems and public and private agencies seems
most likely to result in a continuum of services that can be
accessed by families statewide. There also needs to be a framework through which adoptive families of all types can be fully
informed of available services and how to access them.

Families with serious needs require therapeutic interventions from highly skilled professionals with in-depth knowledge about adoption and the complexity of issues and interventions related to these problem situations. States must
develop their capacity to provide such services to all types of
adoptive families at this level of severe need, even if some services are offered on a sliding-scale payment basis. These families need flexible service delivery that can work in a manner
that goes beyond the typical one-hour weekly office session,
so they can respond quickly in crisis situations, work collabo-
ratively with multiple systems, provide advocacy as needed,
and match the intensity of services to family needs. For any
family with children at risk of maltreatment, placement outside the home, or dissolution, accessible state-supported services are clearly in the child's best interests.

Adoptions Need Ongoing Support

This paper's title, "*Keeping the Promise*," reflects the covenant
that is made between parents and children when adoptions
take place—to be a permanent family. But the covenant is also
between agencies and families and between state or federal
governments and adoptive families whom they help create. In
domestic infant and intercountry adoptions, adoption profes-

sionals have assisted the families in their adoptions, approved them as meeting certain standards through a home study process, and committed to locating, arranging or providing whatever post-adoption supports the families need. For intercountry adopters, the U.S. Citizens and Immigration Services has reviewed the families' documents, including their home studies, to determine that they are suitable to adopt and has approved all U.S. families adopting from foreign countries.

In adoptions from foster care, the state child welfare authority has removed these children from their original families, cared for them for a period of years (sometimes compounding the harm to them), and ultimately selected the families who adopts them with an agreement to provide needed supports over the course of childhood. When families struggle to address the developmental consequences of children's early adversity, they should be entitled to receive the types of services that truly meet their needs and sustain them.

Finally, through a number of laws, the federal government has aggressively supported adoptions from foster care, even providing financial incentives to states to increase their adoptions. The federal government has a role in creating these families and needs to act just as forcefully to sustain them. Only with federal, state, and local partnerships can we truly fulfill the three-fold mission of child welfare: promoting the safety, permanency, and well-being of children.

Organizations to Contact

The editors have compiled the following list of organizations concerned with the issues debated in this book. The descriptions are derived from materials provided by the organizations. All have publications or information available for interested readers. The list was compiled on the date of publication of the present volume; names, addresses, phone and fax numbers, and e-mail and Internet addresses may change. Be aware that many organizations take several weeks or longer to respond to inquiries, so allow as much time as possible.

Bastard Nation
PO Box 1469, Edmond, OK   73083
(415) 704-3166
website: www.bastards.org

Bastard Nation is an advocacy group promoting the rights of adult citizens who were adopted as children. Its primary mission is the restoration of adoptees' rights to access their records. Its publications include fact sheets on various topics as well as *The Basic Bastard: The Bible of Adoptee Rights.*

Center for Adoption Policy (CAP)
168A Kirby Lane, Rye, NY   10580
website: www.adoptionpolicy.org

CAP is an organization that aims to remove barriers to domestic and intercountry adoption. It provides research, analysis, and education to practitioners and the public about current adoption legislation and practices. Its publications include the document "Best Practices in International Adoptions Proposed Framework" and reports such as "Statistics for International Adoptions to the United States for Fiscal Year 2010."

Child Welfare Information Gateway
Children's Bureau/ACYF, Washington, DC   20024
(800) 394-3366
e-mail: info@childwelfare.gov
website: www.childwelfare.gov

The Child Welfare Information Gateway is a service of the Children's Bureau, Administration for Children and Families, US Department of Health and Human Services and is a comprehensive resource on all aspects of adoption. Its services include technical assistance to professionals and policy makers, a library collection, searchable databases on adoption resources, and information on federal and state legislation. Among its publications are free factsheets, issue briefs, and other resources to download or order, including "Adoption Activities on the Internet: A Call for Regulation" and "Ethical Issues in Open Adoption: Implications for Practice."

Dave Thomas Foundation for Adoption
525 Metro Place North, Suite 220, Dublin, OH   43017
(800) 275-3832
e-mail: info@davethomasfoujdation.org
website: www.davethomasfoundation.org

The Dave Thomas Foundation for Adoption is a non-profit public charity dedicated to dramatically increasing the adoptions of the more than 140,000 children in North America's foster care systems. Dave Thomas, founder of Wendy's restaurants, created the Foundation in 1992 to assure that every child has a permanent home and a loving family. The foundation publishes free booklets, including *Finding Forever Families: A Step-by-Step Guide to Adoption* and *Strengthen Your Forever Family: A Step-by-Step Guide to Post-Adoption*.

Evan B. Donaldson Adoption Institute
120 E. 38th St., New York, NY   10016
(212) 925-4089 • fax: (775) 796-6592
e-mail: info@adoptioninstitute.org
website: www.adoptioninstitute.org

The Evan B. Donaldson Adoption Institute is a nonprofit organization dedicated to strengthening adoption policy and practice. The institute conducts research, educates the public, and promotes better policy and the translation of this policy into better adoption practice. Among its numerous publications are Adoption Attitude National Surveys and various policy and practice papers, including *Expanding Resources for Children III: Research-Based Best Practices in Adoption by Gays and Lesbians* and *Never Too Old: Achieving Permanency and Sustaining Connections for Older Youth in Foster Care.*

Foster Care to Success (FCS)
21351 Gentry Dr., Suite 130, Sterling, VA   20166
(571) 203-0270 • fax: (571) 203-0273
website: http://fc2success.org

Founded in 1981, Foster Care to Success is dedicated to supporting the thousands of young people who age out of foster care each year. FCS awards funding to enable these youth to attend college and trade school, and also provides mentoring, academic coaching, internships, and care packages to ensure their graduation and successful entry into the workforce. Its website publishes a blog, fact sheet *FCS News and Events* as well as *Expressions*, a forum for students to contribute personal stories.

Joint Council on International Children's Services (JCICS)
117 South Saint Asaph, Alexandria, VA   22314
(703) 535-8045 • fax:(703) 535-8049
e-mail: info@jointcouncil.org
website: www.jointcouncil.org

The JCICS is the lead voice on intercountry children's services. Its mission is to advocate on behalf of children in need of permanent, safe, and loving families. The council promotes ethical child welfare practices, strengthens professional standards, and educates adoptive families, social service professionals, and government representatives throughout the world. Its website publishes the blog *Be the Answer for Children* and provides links to various news and informational articles.

National Council for Adoption (NCFA)

225 N. Washington St., Alexandria, VA   22314-2561
(703) 299-6633 • fax: (703) 299-6004
e-mail: ncfa@adoptioncouncil.org
website: www.adoptioncouncil.org

The National Council for Adoption advocates for the positive option of adoption while promoting the well-being of children, birth parents, and adoptive families. NCFA is a research, education, and advocacy organization. The council publishes the monthly *Adoption Advocate*, the *National Adoption Report*, and the *Adoption Factbook*.

National Family Justice Association (NFJA)

PO Box 35, Hubbard, OH   44425
e-mail: nfjainfo@aol.com
website: www.nfja.org

The NFJA's goal is to provide information about laws and policies that are negatively affecting American families. NFJA advocates reform in such areas as parental abduction, unjust adoptions, and fraudulent paternity establishments. It publishes position statements and articles on these and other issues.

National Foster Care Coalition (NFCC)

605 North Carolina Ave., SE, Unit #2, Washington, DC   20003
(202) 280-2039
website: www.nationalfostercare.org

The National Foster Care Coalition aims to improve the lives of children, youth, and adults in and from foster care. The coalition advocates on behalf of children and families involved in foster care, supports foster care initiatives, and offers training and education about foster care to policy makers. Its publications include the reports "Supporting Grandparents and Relative Caregivers," and "Resources to Find Families and Prepare Foster Youth for Adulthood."

North American Council on Adoptable Children (NACAC)
970 Raymond Ave., Suite 106, St. Paul, MN   55114
(651) 644-3036 • fax: (651) 644-9848
e-mail: info@nacac.org
website: www.nacac.org

The NACAC is an organization dedicated to waiting children and the families who adopt them. It promotes and supports permanent placement of children and youth in the United States and Canada, especially those in foster care and with special needs. NACAC publishes the quarterly newsletter *Adoptalk* as well as other publications, such as *It's Time to Make Older Child Adoption a Reality: Because Every Child and Youth Deserves a Family* and *Voices from the Heart: Personal Stories from Adoptive Families.*

Pact—An Adoption Alliance
4179 Piedmont Avenue, Suite 101, Oakland, CA   94611
(510) 243-9460 • fax: (510) 243-9970
e-mail: info@pactadopt.org
website: www.pactadopt.org

Pact is a nonprofit organization with a primary mission to serve children of color in need of adoption or who are growing up in adoptive families. They believe that offering the best resources to adoptive parents is in the child's best interests to help them cope with a world whose attitudes too often reflect "adoptism" and racism. Among the organizations many publications are the manual *Nuts & Bolts of Adoption* and the magazine *Pact Press*, which includes such articles as "Open Adoption" and "Talking with Kids about Adoption."

Bibliography

Books

David Archuletta   *Odyssey of an Unknown Father: The Complete Book on Wrongful Adoption.* Tucson, AZ: Wheatmark, 2008.

Susan Bennett   *Late Discoveries: An Adoptee's Quest for Truth.* McKinleyville, CA: Daniel & Daniel Publishers, 2011.

David M. Brodzinsky and Adam Pertman   *Adoption by Lesbians and Gay Men: A New Dimension in Family Diversity.* New York: Oxford University Press, 2012.

Teresa A. Brown   *Adoption Records Handbook.* Las Vegas: Crary Publications, 2008.

Bunny Crumpacker and J.S. Picariello   *Jessica Lost: A Story of Birth, Adoption, and the Meaning of Motherhood.* New York: Union Square Press, 2011.

Mary Ann Davis   *Children for Families or Families for Children: The Demography of Adoption Behavior in the U.S.* New York: Springer, 2011.

Karen Dubinsky   *Babies Without Borders: Adoption and Migration Across the Americas.* New York: New York University Press, 2010.

Amy Ford   *Brown Babies, Pink Parents.* Providence, RI: Triple M Productions, 2010.

Jennifer A. Fort

Created: A Gift for Birthmothers of Open Adoption. United Kingdom: Perfect Publishers, Ltd., 2011.

Bruce Gillespie and Lynne Van Luven

Somebody's Child: Stories About Adoption. Victoria, British Columbia: Touchwood Editions, 2011.

Annabel Goodyer

Child-Centered Foster Care: A Rights-Based Model for Practice. Philadelphia: Jessica Kingsley Publishers, 2011.

Matthew W. Hoffman and Krista Hoffman

Hattie's Advocate: Adopting a Family Through Foster Care. Mohegan Lake, NY: Demarche Publishing LLC, 2011.

Arleta James

Brothers and Sisters in Adoption: Helping Children Navigate Relationships when New Kids Join the Family. Indianapolis: Perspectives Press, 2009.

Mark C. Jerng

Claiming Others: Transracial Adoption and National Belonging. Minneapolis: University of Minnesota Press, 2010.

Eleana J. Kim

Adopted Territory: Transnational Korean Adoptees and the Politics of Belonging. Durham, NC: Duke University Press, 2010.

Ellen Lewin

Gay Fatherhood: Narratives of Family and Citizenship in America. Chicago: University of Chicago Press, 2009.

Diana Marre and Laura Briggs — *International Adoption: Global Inequalities and the Circulation of Children.* New York: New York University Press, 2009.

Russell D. Moore — *Adopted for Life: The Priority of Adoption for Christian Families & Churches.* Wheaton, IL: Crossway Books, 2009.

Kristen A. Morton — *With One Heart: A Guide to Building Relationships Between Birth and Adoptive Mothers in Open Adoption.* CreateSpace, 2011.

John Rosati and Kelly Rosati — *Wait No More: One Family's Amazing Adoption Journey.* Carol Stream, IL: Tyndale House Publishers, 2011.

Marlou Russell — *Adoption Wisdom: A Guide to the Issues and Feelings of Adoption.* Santa Monica, CA: Broken Branch Productions, 2010.

Darron T. Smith, Cardell K. Jacobsen, Brenda G. Juarez, and Joe R. Feagin — *White Parents, Black Children: Experiencing Transracial Adoption.* Lanham, MD: Rowman & Littlefield, 2011.

Barbara Yngvesson — *Belonging in an Adopted World: Race, Identity, and Transnational Adoption.* Chicago: University of Chicago Press, 2010.

Periodicals and Internet Resources

Janna J. Annest   "Is Open Adoption Right for Your Family?" AdoptiveFamilies.com, 2011.

Gabrielle Banks   "Breaking Down Open Adoptions," *Pittsburgh Post Gazette*, December 13, 2010.

Child Welfare Information Gateway   "The Rights of Unmarried Fathers," www.ChildWelfare.gov, 2010.

Angie Chuang   "Haiti's 'Orphans' and the Transracial Adoption Dilemma," TheRoot.com, February 9, 2010.

Ron Claiborne and Hanna Siegel   "Transracial Adoption Can Provide a Loving Family and an Identity Struggle," ABCNews.go.com, March 3, 2010.

Tony Dokoupil   "Raising Katie: What Adopting a White Girl Taught a Black Family About Race in the Obama Era," *Newsweek*, April 22, 2009.

Raquel Ellis, Karin Malm, and Erin Bishop   "The Timing of Termination of Parental Rights: A Balancing Act for Children's Best Interests," *Child Trends Research Brief*, www.ChildTrends.org, September 2009.

Jean Nelson
Erichsen

"Protecting the Rights of
Intercountry Adoptees: Steps to
Ensure the Right of Citizenship for
Every Adopted Individual," *Adoption
Advocate* No. 40, National Council
for Adoption, October 2011.

Rachel H. Farr
and Charlotte J.
Patterson

"Transracial Adoption by Lesbian,
Gay, and Heterosexual Couples: Who
Completes Transracial Adoptions and
with What Results?" *Adoption
Quarterly*, 12:187–204, August 10,
2009.

Jesse Fruhwirth

"Some Call It Kidnapping: How Utah
Adoption Laws Take Babies from the
Nation's Unmarried Fathers," *Salt
Lake City Weekly*, July 28, 2010.

Jane Ganahl

"No Partner? No Problem, When
Adopting a Child," SecondAct.com,
June 9, 2011.

H. Fields Grenee

"Unraveling the Black Adoption
Myths in America," AtlantaPost.com,
August 15, 2011.

Jeanne Howard
and Madelyn
Freundlich

"Expanding Resources for Waiting
Children II: Eliminating Legal and
Practice Barriers to Gay and Lesbian
Adoption from Foster Care," Evan B.
Donaldson Adoption Institute,
September 2008.

Independent
Adoption Center

"Open Adoption," AdoptionHelp.org,
Spring 2010.

John Johnston	"Drop in International Adoptions Sparks Debate," *The Cincinnati Enquirer*, July 25, 2011.
Jeninne Lee-St. John	"Should Race Be a Factor in Adoptions?" *Time*, May 27, 2008.
Jerry Markon	"'Baby Emma' Case Puts State Adoption Laws Between Father, Child," *Washington Post*, April 14, 2010.
New York Times	"Celebrity Adoptions and the Real World," May 10, 2009.
Andrea Poe	"Adopting Older Children: Resources Are Too Few, but Are Out There," *The Washington Times*, April 11, 2011.
Katherine Quamby	"Transracial Adoption: Is Love Enough?" HuffingtonPost.com, February 13, 2011.
Mario Salazar	"Foster Children Need Loving Homes," *The Washington Times*, September 16, 2011.
Erik L. Smith	"What Birth Fathers Don't Know Hurts Everyone," Adoption.com, 2003.
Marc Zappala	"On the Benefits of a National Putative Father Registry," *Adoption Advocate* No. 14, National Council for Adoption, June 2009.

Elizabeth Zavala   "Immigration Nightmare: Adopted and Deported," *Forth Worth Star-Telegram*, January 9, 2010.

Index